ONE WOMAN'S PLACE

A MEMOIR

Donna Schilling

ONE WOMAN'S PLACE

ISBN: 978-0-9890478-1-4

Printed and bound in the United States of America
Cover and interior design by Marlene Wisuri
Dovetailed Press LLC

Cover photographs by
Kathryn Nordstrom Studios
Marlene Wisuri

All photos are from the collection of
Donna Schilling except where noted.

Lakewalk Press
2 N. 58th Ave. East #101
Duluth, Minnesota 55804
218-525-1012

ACKNOWLEDGMENTS

My thanks and appreciation to Marlene Wisuri for sharing her artistic gifts in designing the exterior and interior of *One Woman's Place*, and guiding me through its publication. It exceeds my expectations.

To my special friends, Mara Kirk Hart and Dr. Judy Nelson, I express my gratitude for their careful reading, unending patience, thoughtful encouragement, and suggestions that helped bring the stories to life.

To my loving daughter, Dawn Schilling, dear friends, Joan Smith and Cornelia Dacey, I am deeply grateful for their many hours of careful attention to proofreading. I also thank Cornelia for the suggestion of *One Woman's Place* as I struggled to find the book's final title.

To the trio who worked with me diligently for the past two years to finalize our projects, Martha Aas, Erin O'Daniel, and Elizabeth Preston, I offer my thanks for your faithful presence and careful critique.

I thank the Lake Superior Writers Sunday Memoir group for their attention to my reading and their many fine suggestions over the past several years.

My appreciation to Phil Mickelson for permission to use his history of the Little Yellow Ski-Doo, and to Jerry Calengor for his time and interest in the Snow Business segment.

I am grateful for the friendship of Katherine Coventry, who has supported my work since we attended our first writing class together. As of this year, at age one hundred, she continues to inspire me with her writing.

Author's Note: The stories in *One Woman's Place* are true to the best of my knowledge or memory. Occasionally names have been changed where memory fails, or to avoid offending characters included in the contents.

This book is dedicated to

MARA KIRK HART

Photo by Kathryn Nordstrom Studios

ONE WOMAN'S PLACE - CONTENTS

PART 1 - DISCOVERIES — 10
A Woman's Place — 11
Magic Portal — 14
The Departure — 17
OPS - A New Agency — 27

PART 2 - NEW BEGINNINGS — 28
Ingenue' — 29
Clarice — 31
Working With Others — 34
Unwitting Benefactor — 36

PART 3 - A TEMPTING OFFER — 38
Time Out — 39
Breaking Loose — 42
Options — 43
Revelations — 45

PART 4 - BANK CAPERS — 48
Bulls and Bears — 49
Harbingers of Change — 53
Painful Transition — 56
On Promoting Efficiency — 59
Hi-Jinx — 61
Gender Gap — 64
A Time to Move On — 66
Interlude — 70

PART 5 - SNOW BUSINESS — 74
23 Skidoo — 75
Burgeoning Technology — 80
Meeting the Sales Reps — 90
Return to Montreal — 97
Vintage Ski-Doo History — 98

PART 6 - LIFE AT ENTERPRISES   102

A Voice From the Past   103
Behind the Double Doors   104
What About Bob?   109

PART 7 - GRANDMA'S, INC.   114

A Lateral Move   115
Grandma's Marathon   118
Grandma's II   129

PART 8 - A CORNER STORE   140

The Plan   141
Preparation   142
Under Control   144
Deadline Respite   146
The Reality   148
The Staff   154
A Wise Decision   159

PART 9 - PINNACLES   162

Aftermath   163
On the Threshold of 2000   165
New Millennium - New Life   166
A Year of Loss   167
Rocky Mountain High   171

PREFACE

    This story of a search for one woman's place in the world was inspired on a spring day in 2009 during lunch with friends at Chester Creek Cafe in Duluth, Minnesota.

    We were talking about our work experiences when a member of the group inquired, "Donna, why haven't you written anything about your working life. What did you do before you were a writer?"

    At seventy-five, I was older than the others by fifteen or twenty years, and I laughed as I replied, "I thought it was too mundane a subject to interest anyone. I worked in business offices and banks—I'm a throwback to the 1950s-1980s; the days when a company president could give an indulgent chuckle and say things like: "We can't assign this kind of responsibility to women; you know they run off on us to have babies."

    "But that isn't even legal. Did someone really say that to you. Didn't anyone sue in those days?"

    This explosive response took me aback. Then I realized that, at their ages, my friends were unlikely to remember that women had no recourse against the insulting discrimination existing just a few decades ago: unfair pay scales, lack of benefits, and general disrespect.

    When I referred to "a throwback to earlier decades," I was recalling the skills and equipment I worked with in those years; Gregg shorthand and a parade of typewriters, Dictaphones, calculators, teletypes, electronic word processing typewriters, rotary dial phones—all rendered obsolete by rapid advances in technology. This was the backdrop against which my generation of office workers played our roles. Within a few decades, the skills and machinery that took me into the world of business in 1951 had been replaced by computer technology.

    Our lively question and answer session around the lunch table that day in 2009 included comments by the younger women about their experiences in today's world; jobs of real substance, legal remedies to combat discrimination, and a new acceptance of women's status. Our conversation ended with, "You should write about this, Donna."

The following pages are my response to that challenge and the story of how I reinvented myself throughout my working years and beyond. With the unwitting help of long-gone John Gregg, creator of the shorthand style I continue to use, I tailored that skill to a new purpose in a business world struggling to catch up with galloping technological advances.

I begin the story by looking back to recall how my own attitudes and decisions were formed, setting me on a course that led me through a parade of business offices, self-employment, then finally to my secret love—writing.

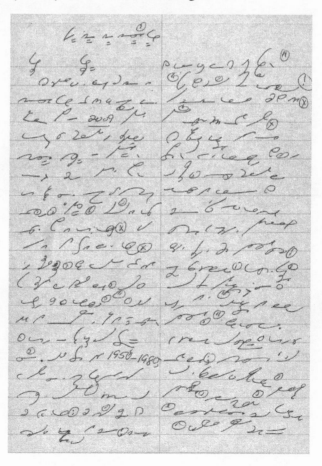

PART 1

DISCOVERIES

A Woman's Place

I had been married over thirty years when I unearthed the small shiny ceramic figure finished in muted pastels tucked away in a box of memorabilia left by my husband's grandmother. It depicted a woman in an ankle length skirt carrying a basket that covered her entire upper body. A motto emblazoned across the front of the basket read, "Man works from sun to sun—Woman's work is never done," a familiar old adage supposedly defining the role of women in the twentieth century. The inscription on the basket had never reflected my view of a woman's role, but it started me thinking about how I had developed my ideas of a woman's place in the world.

The discovery took me back to my early years, reminding me of my mother. I had heard the quote of the basket's message from her lips more than once, evidence that it was accepted by a number of her generation as their "lot in life." To Mother, it fit in with Original Sin and, along with childbirth, part of the retribution meted out when Eve succumbed to the wiles of the serpent. Mother's fundamental religious belief based on biblical scripture, uncompromisingly ruled her life, and subsequently her children's early years. When I was a child, she had used the beginning of the quote "Man works from sun to sun..." to remind us that poor Daddy works long hours out in the cold to make a living.

When it came to the second half of the quote, "...woman's work is never done," she evidently considered his wife and children, privileged to stay home and invest whatever time and effort was required to make him feel like a king—and life in his "castle" idyllic.

11

As I was growing up, my Aunt Alma became a role model who continued to exert a positive influence on me throughout her life and beyond. I admired her for being her own person, confident in her own competence. I expected to continue to learn and grow as she had. It didn't occur to me that society would impose rules, short of applying force, to contain me in my gender role. I always felt like a person, rather than a pawn to be controlled by others who prevailed simply by accident of gender. Mother considered that attitude willful, and I'm sure prayed diligently to save my immortal soul.

My "Alma Watching" began as a five-year-old preschooler. I saw a single woman approaching middle age who was self-sufficient and industrious. She set out to fulfill her determination that she and her younger siblings would have better opportunities than their Norwegian immigrant parents had known. She left home at

Aunt Alma P. Heieie at White Bear Lake, Minnesota, ca. 1930.

fourteen to live in Badger, Minnesota, the nearest town with a high school, to continue her education, caring for children and helping with housework in exchange for room and board. Her journal from those days contained the following telling note, "Olette and Hannah (sisters) came down and stayed at Larson's overnight, the only two from home that could make it for the graduation."

Following high school, her journal goes on to say, "In 1911, Hannah and I attended teacher's training school at Roseau, Minnesota. Hannah was married in June, so I returned to school alone. I celebrated my eighteenth birthday on Sept 22, 1912..."

Earning tuition through summer work, she completed her teacher's training and returned to the small Greenbush, Minnesota, country school near her hometown to teach grades one through eight. Although the family spoke Norwegian at home, Alma had taught her younger siblings (including my mother) to speak English and, subsequently, basic reading, writing, and arithmetic in the local one-room rural school.

Alma's siblings included my Uncle Marion, the youngest and the only boy in the family. Her main concern after seeing her other younger siblings through the eighth grade, was to see that Marion attended the University of Minnesota to prepare for a profession. This would require more than a teacher's salary. To accomplish her goal, she combined her household management skills with her organizational ability earning her a position as manager of a wealthy household in White Bear Lake, Minnesota.

Uncle Marion T. Heieie as a student at the University of Minnesota, Minneapolis, ca. 1936.

Uncle Marion graduated from the university's school of dentistry and practiced in Minnetonka until his retirement. From early childhood, I was aware of Marion's artistic talent, particularly in water color. In writing this now, I feel certain the subject of his art was probably never mentioned to the pragmatic Alma as a possible pursuit of study. In his retirement years, he used the bounty from his flower gardens as subjects for the water colors he created until well past his ninetieth year. I stayed in touch with Uncle Marion and his wife through the years, and know he would be pleased to find me pursuing what I believed was my true calling.

In time, Alma bought a home for herself in Wayzata, Minnesota, where she lived with her older sister Olette. When her parents gave up their farm, she established them in a home in Monticello, Minnesota.

Alma accepted each member of our family for who we were, but Mother was not able to accept Alma's choices and often expressed disapproval of her sister, based on her decision to remain single and childless. Quoting from the Bible, Mother proclaimed it was the Lord's will that women marry and have children. Although I felt conflicted and disloyal to Mother, I could not help thinking it was unfair of her to pass judgment on the aunt I adored. She had been raised in the same ultra-strict Norwegian Lutheran environment as Mother, but she eschewed the dire warnings of hellfire and brimstone. Although a faithful church goer, the Golden Rule was more suited to her belief system than the harsh tenets of her childhood religion.

Aunt Alma gave me a new notion of what a woman's place could be, but I know instinctively that this practical woman's scope could not have harbored thoughts of my uncle as an artist or me as a writer. It would have been totally out of step with her time and circumstance.

Magic Portal

Convinced that the written word held the key to unlock any door to the knowledge I craved—I pursued whatever subjects beckoned me, and continue to do so. My older sister, Wanda had taught me the alphabet "playing school." She assumed the attitude of her teacher saying, "Today class (that was me) we will learn to write ABCs. Please print each one ten times."

I thought she was awfully bossy, but my eagerness to learn overcame my objection to her methods. In September 1939, at six years of age, I followed Wanda and our older brother Jerry on shortcuts through stubbly cornfields, intimidated by the prospect of being the youngest student in all eight grades.

As I crossed the threshold of Lake Beauty, stepping through the magic portal into the world of words, Wanda admonished me, "Remember now, you can't talk out loud unless the teacher calls on you." The long awaited day had arrived—I would begin learning to read by myself.

Painstakingly sounding out words in my reader *Fun With Dick and Jane*, which described their simple life, along with their dog Spot, I discovered reading was going to take more patience than I had imagined. The title's promise of *fun* did not live up to the repetitive text of, "See Dick; see Dick run. Run Dick, run. See Jane; see Jane run. Run Jane, run." I found no adventure in the tiresome lines. An immediate benefit, however, that made reading a lifetime blessing was my being the only first grader with the teacher all to myself for my lessons. It was like having a tall, slim, blond private tutor, who taught me to read well. I adored Miss Classman. I soon began writing my own poems, stories and plays in a fat three-by-four inch tablet of rainbow colors, which cost me a precious nickel on a Saturday evening in Long Prairie. My efforts were viewed with scorn by my siblings and amusement by Mother so I never showed them to Daddy, who approved of me. I didn't want to risk his saying something kind, and hearing Mother say, "Lee, don't encourage her in that foolishness!"

But I did share them with *Daddy's* mother who visited us each summer and was interested in my rhymes and stories. When she had read them, she asked, "Do you think I could have these to take home?" Delighted that *someone* liked my writing, I quickly told her, "Sure, Grandma, I can always write more!"

There were few books in our rural home, and our country school library consisted of one meager shelf of books which we were not allowed to take from the building. When I was eight years old, we moved to the small town of Long Prairie, giving me access to a library and all the reading I could handle at that stage of my life. By second grade, I was making good progress in school.

That fateful Sunday in December we had no inkling that we would be leaving our idyllic (albeit Spartan) life. It began as most Sundays did, with Dad driving five miles to a crossroads store to buy the Sunday paper. The usual squabble ensued over the comic section, which we called *funny papers*. "I want *Maggie and Jiggs* first this time." I shouted. "You got them first last Sunday, It's my turn," Wanda claimed. Jerry was demanding *The Katzenjammer Kids* for himself.

"*Quiet!*" Mother's voice held an urgency that stopped us cold. She and Dad had been listening to the battery-operated radio. Because batteries had to be taken to town for recharging, radio use was restricted to a few evening programs and weekend presentations we could all enjoy—*Amos and Andy, Fibber McKee and Molly, Let's Pretend*, and news broadcasts.

Now, the only sound in the room was the voice of Franklin Roosevelt announcing that an unprovoked attack by Japan on Pearl Harbor had drawn the United States into the war—it was December 7, 1941, "A day that would live in infamy," we heard President Roosevelt declare. Hawaii was a United States territory, and the news left American citizens stunned. Although it took some time for my family to feel the full effect of the news, it came sooner than we expected.

Our small rural community didn't change much in the days that followed that first announcement. Our limited sources of news shielded us from the daily barrage of fact and fiction which we sometimes seek to escape today. In our rural farm area, there were no factories to convert to production of war materials so activity remained relatively normal. Word-of-mouth informed us of the departure of local youth to serve in the armed forces.

Blissfully unaware of those form letters which began, "Greetings, you are hereby ordered to report to active duty in the armed forces...." we were, therefore, stunned when these letters were received by my father and brother, members of the Minnesota State Guard, requiring them to report for active duty. Now the reality of the world conflict exploded on my small sphere like a bombshell. What would become of us? A mother left alone with three girls, and my daddy who approved of me just the way I was, and my brother whose teasing suddenly didn't seem so bad, going away...for how long?

The Departure

"When is the bus coming, Daddy?" I asked anxiously. My anxiety stemmed from our awareness that the bus would carry off both my dad and brother, along with the other members of the Long Prairie division of the Minnesota State Guard. On that cold day late in 1942, street dust mixed with fallen leaves swirled around the band of families huddled in front of City Hall, waiting to bid goodbye to loved ones.

"Remember, we won't cry," Mother reminded us quietly. She had privately urged us to smile bravely and wave so Daddy and Jerry would feel it was okay to leave us—it was *that kind of war with everyone knowing the stakes were huge.* When we found Dad was leaving, however, Mother's chin-up resolution was strained to its limit. She uncharacteristically delivered an ultimatum. "We *will* be moving to Long Prairie. I have no intention being left with three young girls by ourselves out here in the sticks," she had declared in the tone of voice that left no room for discussion.

Father, Pvt. William Lee Ferdon at Twin Ponds in Duluth, 1943.

She and Dad found a house for rent and we were settled before he had to leave for the city of Duluth on Lake Superior, the setting for my favorite poem, Longfellow's *Hiawatha*. The Minnesota State Guard was mobilized to protect its port of Duluth and the ore-rich Iron Range which sent its treasure to be shipped down the Great Lakes and turned into weapons of war. When we discovered that Duluth was the destination of the Long Prairie State Guard unit, I breathed a little easier. I had, in my limited knowledge of the war, pictured Dad and Jerry in the midst of fighting somewhere in Europe.

I had entered third grade in our Lake Beauty country school, and we moved at the end of the first semester, so we began Long Prairie school mid-term. I loved being in town. There were playmates close to home and a school where I learned to read music. Our art classes combined with social studies to create a series of dioramas depicting scenes from the lives of children around the world. Sturdy cardboard boxes provided the bases, cleverly disguised by a variety of colorful material. There was a library close to the school where we could borrow as many books as we could carry, and the librarian became my best friend. She always had time to visit with me and help me find suitable books; *Grimm's Fairy Tales*, *Heidi*, *Black Beauty*, and other favorites.

Lady, a faithful Water Spaniel with brown and white silky curls, watched over my sisters and me as we played and accompanied us to the pharmacy a few blocks from home. There, medicinal smells combined with perfumes and cosmetics, but best of all, the delectable aroma of penny candy, to create a heady atmosphere. These confections, like magnets, drew the "silver" pennies from our pockets (not real silver but a substitute for the copper essential to the war). For a few cents we could bring home a little brown bag of penny candy. We agonized over our choices, leaving our fingerprints on the polished glass case as we peered at the enticing array of sweets until the clerk finally said, "You'll have to make up your minds. I have other work to do."

Forced to decide, we usually settled on candy cigarettes and tiny sealed wax bottles of flavored juice that we called "champagne." Careful to stay out of sight of Mother, we felt elegantly sophisticated with our sickly sweet cigarettes and waxy "champagne." Enchanted by the Saturday night movies we occasionally saw at the small Long Prairie theater, we tried to emulate the glamorous stars of the early 1940s puffing away while sipping their wine. Bette Davis was particularly artful at using these props effectively, and we tried to imitate her by striding about waving our cigarettes as we delivered our favorite quote from the romantic film, *Now Voyager*, "Oh Jerry...Let's don't ask for the moon...we have the stars."

We needn't have worried about Mother lecturing us on the evils of tobacco and wine. She was too busy hatching The Plan. Years earlier, when she met Dad, she was living and working in St. Paul, rooming with her older sisters, Alma and Olette. Raised in a remote rural community, she had not expected to return to that life of isolation. Yet, that is exactly where she was by the time I was born. When I grew up, I finally understood that while we were in school for much of the year, Mother had spent long, lonely days in an ill-equipped drafty house without running water or electricity. It was no wonder that she wanted to move to

Mother, Alice O. Ferdon working at Bell switchboard in St. Paul, ca. 1918.

town, and eventually to a larger city where her children could grow up with advantages she had not enjoyed.

Shortly after summer vacation began, she called my sisters and me together and explained The Plan, "Now that school is out, I'm going to visit Daddy and Jerry in Duluth. Grandma will come and stay with you while I'm gone. Daddy only has a two-day pass so I'll be back in a couple of days."

Our amazing mother had somehow eked out enough money to make this trip. The two days seemed endless, and on her return, we were bursting with questions, "How did you like it?

19

Did you see ore boats on the lake?—How big was it?" Mother was a great story teller and she had seen plenty to fire her imagination. We were wide-eyed as she gave us the full benefit of her technique, "The main street is just a speedway, and there are houses stuck all over a hill as big as a mountain so far above the city the houses look like toys." (This was fascinating to kids who had spent their life to date in flat prairie country.)

"The ore boats are long and flat and sound a loud horn when they want to come through the bridge." Now we discovered Phase Two of The Plan. She and Dad had found an upstairs apartment in Duluth and bought the necessary furniture to get us started. "We'll be moving to Duluth as soon as we can sell most of our things."

Wow. We were stunned, but when Mother asked us to help with preparations for the move, we quickly regained our voices and promised to pitch in. "Can I go to the library?" Mother smiled—she knew I was going to pester the librarian for information about Duluth.

I tore to the library to tell my friend the big news. "Guess where we're going? We're moving to Duluth," I announced. She feigned surprise, but since she knew where my father was stationed, it was obvious.

"Let's see if we can find some books with pictures. Do you know much about the city?"

"I know its on Hiawatha's Lake...and mother told us about the hills and boats."

The librarian brought out a couple of books that had pictures of Duluth on its amazing inland sea with the Aerial Bridge, which had been converted to a "lift" bridge around the time I was born, so it was still fairly new in that year of 1943.

The next day, Mother put us to work hand-printing flyers listing the items for sale. She planned to sell furniture and most of the kitchenware, garden tools, and dishes. The limited amount she saved would be sent along with our clothing by truck to Duluth. By the next Saturday our flyers were finished. On Saturdays the farmers came to town for shopping, and Mother sent us downtown to place flyers on or in cars that were parked along Long Prairie's Main Street while their owners' shopped. Crude as they were, the flyers worked. We got rid of everything, including the car. Carrie Hansmeier, the town's antique dealer, did well on her purchases, since Mother placed little value on old collectibles. She liked things to be sparkling new. On July 2, 1943, with the last details attended to, we were packed and ready to leave.

I was nine years old when Mother's careful plans came to fruition. On the way to Little Falls, where we would catch the Greyhound bus, I sat in the front seat between Mother and the first woman driver I had ever ridden with. She was the wife of one of Daddy's fellow servicemen, and I found it fascinating to watch her feet manipulate the pedals of the 1935 black Chevy. I had thought only men drove cars. I wondered if the unshaven, dark haired, muscular legs (which my child's mind perceived as masculine) had something to do with her being adept at driving. I was feeling unsettled about leaving our small town but, listening to her expression of envy at our leaving this part of the state for Duluth, I was somehow comforted, "You are so lucky. I'd love to be moving there myself." At Little Falls she left us to board the Greyhound and begin the journey to our new life.

My experience of places and people beyond our sphere of small lakes, flat prairie countryside, and small towns was non-existent. I had formed opinions from Sunday newspapers and Saturday night movie newsreels featuring brief news summaries of our rapidly changing world. We had seen the front page pictures of Adolph Hitler and his henchmen in the Nazi party with the ever-present black Swastikas, the bombing of Britain, and the troopers goose-stepping across the movie screen with narrators loudly proclaiming increasing Nazi dominance in Germany and adjacent countries. Yet it all seemed so far away until we reached our destination on July 3, 1943.

Nothing had prepared me for the sight as we turned onto Thompson Hill far above the city. I was dazzled when Duluth and Lake Superior came into view with a breathtaking vision of the sun turning the barely rippled water to gold. We entered a city bustling with energy generated by an urgency to produce the raw materials of war, evidenced by smoke pouring from the tall stacks of industrial plants dominating the far western end of the city. We could not begin to imagine the effects of the worldwide conflict on our future; the advances in technology, changes in women's roles, and the resulting accelerated pace.

The reality of life in the confines of a city was a shock and the lake seemed far removed from the upstairs apartment of our crowded neighborhood. (In fact, we were only a few blocks from St. Louis Bay, but Mother certainly wasn't ready for us to undertake exploration of our surrounds.)

The discovery of the Lincoln Library, a branch of the Duluth Public Library downtown, closer to home than the one in Long Prairie was one of my most delightful surprises. It was housed in a charmingly designed brick building and had many more shelves of books than the Long Prairie Library. The librarian had less time to spend with individual kids, but I was becoming familiar with the Dewey Decimal System and soon learned to find my way around the shelves.

Monroe School in my Duluth neighborhood wasn't much different from that of Long Prairie, except for larger classes. I was surprised to find that I was well ahead of my city classmates on the learning curve. Small classes in my early school years had given me the advantage of individual attention by diligent teachers. A few months in the Long Prairie school had heightened my appreciation of art and music. We had poster paints and easels, a variety of colored construction paper, and illustrated books in our art classes in Duluth.

Mr. Johnston, a director of music for the elementary school system, made frequent calls to lead our music class. His favorite number which he projected vigorously in his strong voice was *Mammy's Little Baby Loves Sho'tnin' Bread*, a dubious choice which today would raise valid questions of political correctness.

I was troubled by one thing in my fourth grade class that first year in Duluth. A student named Dale, who was unusually small of stature amused the other kids by playing the class clown to make his presence known. One day the teacher, exasperated by his antics, placed the wastebasket in a front corner of the room, and made Dale stand in it facing the corner for the rest of the class period. The fact that he was small enough to fit in the wastebasket must have made him feel even more diminished by the humiliation of standing there, as a part of the discarded debris, in front of the whole class. We all were

Fourth grade class at Monroe School in Duluth, 1943. Donna is fourth from left, second row.

embarrassed for Dale and ashamed of ourselves for our complicity by laughing at his actions. I liked the teacher, but even at nine years old, I knew the punishment was inappropriate.

I soon became aware that a number of my friends' mothers worked outside the home, replacing men who had enlisted or had been drafted into the armed forces. Mothers didn't hesitate to leave their children with young kids for a few hours. Now I was being asked to "babysit," a term I had never heard in my previous life. I took this responsibility seriously. Although I wasn't thrilled with the duties it entailed, I garnered a fifty-cent piece for those few hours of work, which was much better pay than the penny apiece I received for catching frogs in the pond at Lake Beauty. We would discover when the war ended that many women liked working at jobs which paid regular wages. They weren't eager to give over their jobs to returning servicemen and go back to the kitchen. I didn't realize then that we would not return to our prewar lives.

Some time after Dad finished his two-year obligation in the State Guards, we acquired a set of encyclopedias, a world atlas, and a dictionary, which Dad ordered from a door-to-door salesman. While I was thrilled, Mother was dismayed at the expenditure, frequently commenting on the extravagant twenty-four-dollar price of the dictionary. Wanda still has it in her library, pages now yellowed with age and the leather binding cracked. We still laughingly call it "the twenty-four-dollar job" and, in my opinion, still worth every penny. I was particularly fascinated by its varied information. Printed on thick paper, it was five inches deep and I poured over it, caught up in the endless knowledge I could glean from those pages. I loved words that sounded exactly right for what they described. I still find myself mesmerized by the magic of a quality dictionary when I open it to define a word, and lose myself among its treasures, seeking words with the perfect sound.

Sisters Wanda, Vonnie, and Donna at Lincoln Park, Duluth, 1943.

When I entered East Junior High School, I found it offered students a choice of clubs which met during homeroom session two mornings a week. Attendance was mandatory in our chosen two; mine were journalism and baton twirling. I was already tall in seventh grade, an advantage in basketball and volleyball, the two intramural sports available for girls. These games satisfied my love of team sports. I was growing rapidly, and my gym teacher, Mrs. Keech a former WAC (Women's Army Corps) sergeant, whacked me across the shoulders when I attempted to minimize my height by slumping. I have silently thanked her over the years for this consideration.

By the time I entered Central High School, the war had officially ended. I did not intend to seek a college degree despite the influence of my enterprising Aunt Alma. In my small world women worked as teachers or nurses, and I was convinced I had no disposition for the former and no stomach for the latter. I chose a high school course that continued through the three years I attended Central. I planned to prepare myself with skills required for executive (confidential) secretarial training which could supplement a husband's income or support myself in the event I didn't marry.

The course I chose added an extra dimension to clerical or stenographic work by the extended teaching of office management, poise, and the deportment expected from a secretary assigned to work exclusively for one officer of a company. We were advised on appropriate attire, grooming, and discretion in handling confidential information, as well as when to speak and when to hold back. We were expected to set the tone as an example to the rest of the clerical staff. The demand for executive secretaries was rapidly increasing. They were a mainstay of the busy executives turning postwar corporations from the production of war materials to consumer goods and services. Secretaries to those executives enjoyed an earning potential equivalent to that of administrative assistants in today's business world. I was not interested in other business machines related to bookkeeping or dealing with money. I had no intention of ever getting involved in anything so boring as I perceived that field to be.

My teacher, Miss Golding (we did not address our teachers by first names) gave us periodic dictation tests at eighty, one-hundred, and finally one-hundred-twenty words per minute. We were awarded pins in bronze, silver, and gold engraved with the number of words per minute we had achieved. Eighty words was the lowest passing rate. My 120 WPM gold pin was a reassuring confidence builder with which to face my first job.

Donna's graduation photo, Duluth Central High School, 1951.

Shortly before graduation, Miss Golding asked me to stop after class to inform me of an upcoming job opportunity which would require a civil service test. Having failed to convince me I should continue my education, she suggested I compete for this exceptional opportunity and offered to arrange a release from class time to take the test. I didn't hesitate to take her up on the offer and presented myself at City Hall on the appointed morning, confident in my training and preparation, but aware that qualifications beyond test scores (notably veteran's preference) were used to select candidates. I tried to focus on the work and disregard the large number of hopeful candidates filling the room at City Hall.

Within the week, I received a letter notifying me that I qualified for a job with a new federal government temporary agency soon to open in Duluth. I was elated, but cautioned myself that I still had much to learn.

OPS—A New Agency

In January 1951, President Harry Truman created the Office of Price Stabilization (a temporary federal agency) naming Michael DiSalle, the Mayor of Toledo, Ohio, as its director. Headquartered in Washington D.C., various regional offices were set up to supervise the district offices, one of which was located in Duluth with E. Clifford Mork as its director. This office where I would work was responsible for counties in the northern half of Minnesota, with a regional office in Minneapolis under Phillip Neville's direction.

OPS was created to control prices during the Korean conflict, which began in June of 1950. The forerunner of this agency, the Office of Price Administration, served that purpose in WWII and was also responsible for the rationing of consumer goods, gasoline, and certain food products. Rationing was never introduced during the Korean conflict which was designated a "police action" rather than a war.

As described, OPS was indeed a temporary agency, but I was unaware of just how temporary it would be as I met with the personnel director for my final interview. I learned that I would be assigned to the consumer goods section, which covered the largest number of products subject to price controls. A manager and two assistants headed consumer goods: I was assigned to handle secretarial work. We were responsible for compiling price lists of goods offered by retailers in one section of Minnesota. The goods included hardware, furniture, appliances, and other major household products. I looked forward to meeting the others when I reported to work the next week. Management positions had been filled, their secretaries hired, and they were already on board setting up the office.

On Monday morning I arrived at the Christie Building, my courage bolstered by my tiny gold 120 WPM award hidden as a talisman under the collar of my navy blue "dressmaker" suit. A small matching hat and white cotton gloves, standard accessories for 1951, completed my outfit. I paused for a moment at the door; then took a deep breath before crossing the threshold into my future.

PART 2

NEW BEGINNING

Ingenue'

My eyes took in the cavernous interior of the first floor of the old building undergoing remodeling to accommodate the new OPS agency. I approached the receptionist, who also handled the switchboard; "I'm here to see Mr. Mahnke. I'm starting work today." She buzzed his intercom and waved me into his office. He greeted me and introduced me to the staff. They were mostly welcoming, but I was soon keenly aware that I was alone in my lack of work experience, the youngest person in the agency. I had a flashback to twelve years ago as the only first grader, the youngest kid in school. At this point, all my preparation for office decorum fell away, except for the instinctive use of discretion, which suggested listening as a good stand-in for the self-assurance I lacked.

As a clerk stenographer II, I was responsible for all correspondence, filing, and voluminous form typing (government agencies love forms). A manual prescribing procedures in detail was distributed from Washington to the Minneapolis regional office, and finally to the Duluth district office. The first pages barely arrived before amendments followed in directives from Washington. Amendments were still hot off the press when more directives arrived with revisions to the amendments.

There was one lone woman officer who held the title of "Information Officer." Her job was to corral and distribute all those procedures and revisions. I found her less than cordial, in fact downright rude. As I was introduced to her, she said nothing, but eyed me up and down before declaring, "I used to look like you do, but just wait until you're my age; you won't be so slim and trim either." Even as I bit my tongue and forced a smile acknowledging the introduction, I silently resolved that *I would never look or speak as she did no matter how old I got!*

It would be some years before photocopiers were perfected, and procedures dictated that all correspondence must be typed on one original of heavy bond letterhead, with five carbon copies for distribution to files. The first onion skin copy was white, followed by four in pastel colors of yellow, green, peach, and blue, with sheets of carbon between each copy. We used Smith-Corona manual typewriters, and a heavy touch was necessary to produce clearly printed carbons. Errors were corrected by use of an eraser, with small pieces of paper inserted between *all those sheets of carbon and each copy,* to control smudging. Then having discreetly erased the blight from the original (taking great pains to prevent gouging a hole in the bond paper) corrections were made on each subsequent copy, carefully removing the guard pieces between each page. More than one erasure per page, or a hole in the original, were unacceptable and the whole shebang was scrapped. My mind was boggled by the resulting waste of time and materials, and I silently blessed the typing teachers who had trained me well.

As I became acquainted with the other secretaries in the agency, I found them to be friendly and helpful. The Price Director's secretary Clarice took me under her wing and introduced me to the executive secretaries. Their informal guidance led me through the quagmire of office politics. We shared lunch breaks and social activities after hours, sometimes including husbands and boyfriends. Hartley and I had been married that spring at a small wedding attended by friends and extended families. We lived in an apartment in my east end neighborhood of familiar surroundings. Most of our friends

Donna and Hartley, wedding day, 1951.

were still single, and we seemed to have more in common with our married workmates. Hartley was popular among the OPS people, and we were invited to the mixed activities.

Clarice

I last saw Clarice when she returned to visit Duluth in the later 1950s and brought her five-year-old son, Peter to see me. Recently, I was reminded of this when I ran across a photo of her with her new baby daughter I had received in the mail a year after that visit. It prompted me to see if I could locate her via the internet, in spite of the fifty-year lapse in communication. My efforts to trace her confirmed that neither Clarice nor her husband, Berry was still living. I was not surprised, but it was a sad reminder of how quickly life passes.

Clarice's friendship was an unexpected gift bestowed on me as a rank beginner of eighteen, when she was in her mid-thirties. Of medium height with a trim figure, her carriage and compelling presence made her appear taller. Her auburn pageboy hair style and expressive hazel eyes were enhanced by discreet makeup and a wardrobe dominated by complementary shades of green, gold, and brown. She was openly admired by most of the other women, who instinctively turned to her for advice on everything from office protocol to clothing and makeup. I sometimes heard bits of their conversations in the ladies room where these discussions often took place.

From my side of the office, I admired her appearance as well as her efficiency and intelligence, not expecting to become personally acquainted with her. I was amazed when one day shortly after I started my job, she approached my desk. "We're going out for lunch today; would you like to join us?" The "we" were the other executive secretaries and, flattered by the invitation, I found my voice and accepted.

I quickly learned there was an innate kindness and consideration for others behind Clarice's sophisticated polish; and so we became friends. I became one of the "intimates" among these women, who relied on Clarice's flair for tips on fashion and style. One day, she produced a pair of earrings from her purse saying, "Donna, I think these would be perfect for you, and I have another very similar pair, so I'd like you to have them." And they were just the right style for me. Another time, it was the perfect scarf. I wonder now if she was remembering a young Clarice who had benefitted from the guidance of a mentor on *her* first job. I understood that she was offering me advice, but always tactfully as suggestions, therefore never resented. I recognized that she had years of experience to share and I paid close attention.

She drew me into the group of friends she had attracted—Marlowe, Betty, Myrna, Tyzie, and Gail—who knew their way around business offices, and gradually I developed confidence in my position. Her competence and professional manner was not lost on the men, some of whom felt intimidated. A few women in the office envied Clarice and criticized everything from her marital status to her wardrobe. She was creative in finding shortcuts through the confusion of government red tape and circumventing time-wasting directives in the manual. (I concluded this skill was cultivated by her military administrative experience.)

Clarice was engaged to marry Colonel Berresford Walker, the commander of our local National Guard unit. Berry lived on the second floor of a quaint old building on Superior Street, a few blocks from the apartment where I lived with my husband. When Clarice and Berry married, she moved into his apartment, and the four of us spent time together on evenings and weekends. None of our close friends had married yet and, despite our age difference from the Walkers, it was comfortable to associate with them and some of our other married workmates. We missed their company sorely when Berry received a new assignment the year after they were married.

In the relatively brief time we knew Clarice and Berry, we shared simple pleasures of picnics on the North Shore or evenings visiting at home, often prevailing on Berry to share stories of his military career. His father had also been a career military man so we heard second-hand tales of World War I history, as well as Berry's own experiences. He and Hartley liked each other, and developed a companionable rapport. Clarice and Berry's influence helped smooth the transition for Hartley and me into adulthood.

Clarice's WWII experience in the Women's Army Corps (WACs) was unusual when compared to the number of women active in today's military. She often shared stories of army life with us on lunch and coffee breaks. She said it was generally more monotonous than dangerous or enlightening, working in a khaki world of makeshift offices or as a jeep driver for high ranking personnel. Uniform was mandatory on all occasions except for the hat, which could be removed when off-duty.

"Didn't you have any fun?" Marlowe asked one day at lunch.

"Oh, we had dances and parties to boost morale," Clarice laughed, as she began a story featuring a cocktail hat (a style popular in the 1940s). She created the hat, to wear for a USO dance, from a Chore Boy woven metallic pot scrubber filched from the mess kitchen. Stretched into a circle of attractive copper mesh and secured with bobby pins, it became a sparkling authentic looking beanie. This amusing tale of WAC lore gave me a sense of her resourcefulness and her good-humored refusal to completely surrender *every* shred of femininity to the army. If any vestige of military training clung to her during the transition back to civilian life, it was a significant poise grounded in discipline and confidence.

After the war, during 1945 and 1946, her WAC career culminated in her most engaging assignment when she was sent to Nuremberg, Germany to serve as a court reporter at the war criminal trials of twenty-four Nazis. Clarice was a good narrator, and we listened with rapt attention as she related her participation in this chilling closure to the Nazi reign of terror, a chapter in international history so infamous that vestiges of the shadow it cast on a war-weary world still remain. We marveled that Clarice had sat through that historic tribunal with people we had seen in past years goose-stepping across the screen in newsreels and the front pages of newspapers; people who had committed unspeakable crimes against humanity, and were being called on to account for their actions. I asked Clarice, "How could you focus on your work in that atmosphere?"

"That was about five years ago, and their presence seemed to permeate the courtroom with a chill of evil. The demands—the exacting concentration required to record the proceedings accurately saw us through. It totally consumed our time and energy to focus on the words rather than the deeds of the defendants."

She returned to the United States following her discharge and settled in Texas where she worked for Sun Oil. After a disappointing marriage, which ended in divorce, she returned to her parents' home in Duluth and soon was employed by the agency where I met her.

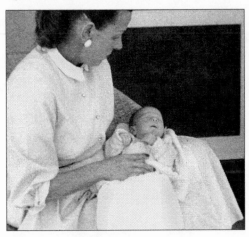

Clarice Walker with her new daughter. ca. 1956.

We exchanged Christmas greetings for a few years before the Walkers were assigned to Germany and we lost touch. Clarice will remain in my heart as one of life's great gifts—a true and loving friend, whose guidance and example influenced my personal as well as my professional development.

Working With Others

Although the Christie Building where I worked was only a half-mile from the classroom cocoon of my high school, the atmosphere was as far removed as Mars. Unlike the classroom where we were all on an equal footing, the business office was inhabited by adults endowed with varying levels of authority. I found myself tentatively negotiating a labyrinth of these co-workers' egos and eccentricities, confident only in the skills I had acquired through training.

Howard, my section manager, was an easy-going, middle-aged man who had previously sold furniture in a retail business, which left him ill-prepared for his management role. He made few demands on his subordinates and spent most of the time sitting at his desk looking contemplative. His most memorable characteristic was a hyena-like laugh which ended in a snort; oddly his laugh never quite reached the near-sighted brown eyes that peered out from horn-rimmed lenses below slightly greying hair.

Paul, one of his assistants, was a younger man recently graduated from college. With pale blond hair and tilted eyes as blue as a Nordic glacier, his dress and grooming were impeccable. He took his job seriously, applying himself in a professional manner, which made him a most satisfactory workmate. I believe that Paul and I were responsible for most of our section's productivity.

Ed was our second assistant manager. I can't claim that his multi-paged letters and memos represented productivity. He liked to be noticed as he bounced through the office, his jaunty walk exuding energy. To assure maximum attention, he occasionally punctuated his movements with an arrogant toss of an ample crown of dark curls. I guessed he was in his mid-thirties and was making the most of his first opportunity to dress in a suit and sit in an office with feet propped on his desk, dictating letters to a secretary. I decided he had probably seen too many *His Girl Friday* movies. He appeared to enjoy the image increasingly as he got the hang of it.

I had been on the job a few weeks when Mary, a clerk typist was added to our section to help with general typing and filing. Ludicrous as it seemed to me, my stenographer status qualified me to supervise this woman old enough to be my mother, who was good-humored about our situation. When her husband died leaving her with high-school age twin sons to support, she had taken a typing course to prepare for her return to work. Endowed with years of life experience, enhanced by good common sense, she was a capable and willing worker who didn't need direction, and we worked companionably together. Without the deluge of filing generated by Ed's effusive output, we would not have needed the extra help, and I was pleased for Mary's sake that she had been the one hired for this well-paid position. Aware of Ed's demands on my time, she cast sympathetic glances in my direction, but said nothing while doing her part to keep our section running smoothly.

Unwitting Benefactor

I was being held hostage to Ed's ego, and many days at closing time I was left with a shorthand pad full of "cold" notes to start my next workday. A number of shorthand symbols have more than one meaning, and accurate transcription relies heavily on the stenographer's grasp of the writing's subject and memory of its content. This meant that notes left overnight presented a challenge that fortunately I was up to. I was blessed with excellent recall, and my habit of writing clean, classic Gregg shorthand. Along with Clarices's recommendation to create personal abbreviations tailored to my specific work, my notes were easy to read. By using small, precisely formed symbols, I saved time, increasing efficiency.

I attacked the full notebook every morning while Ed tuned up for the afternoon by thumbing through trade journals seeking grist for his insatiable dictation mill. I bided my time, and several months later (wheels turned slowly in this typical government agency) someone or something tipped off the Price Director. Perhaps it was the outbox on my desk, an overflowing rainbow of onion skin copies (five per page of Ed's lengthy missives) or perhaps someone discretely mentioned his daily dictation exhibition. It came to a head when I was summoned to my manager's office, where he instructed me to advise Ed that he needed to cut down on the length of his letters and memos. He added in his halting nasal voice that I should also tell him that all mail from our section would be reviewed by the Price Director before being dispatched. It took a minute for his meaning to register—then in a burst of horror, it dawned on me—he really expected *me* to deliver this message; a dilemma for any secretary, let alone an eighteen-year-old novice. Afraid to refuse, I followed Howard's orders.

Trying to be tactful, I approached Ed saying, "Howard asked me to tell you that we need to shorten *our* writings, according to orders from the Price Director." He leapt from his chair and lashed out at me with dark eyes flashing, "Who do you think you are," the tirade began, "telling me what I can and can't write. I don't have to take this!"

It didn't surprise me; he was humiliated, and I understood his reaction, which was in keeping with his personality. I had to admire his audacity when he huffed off to confront Howard regarding his secondhand order, but I was relieved that Ed's journal-quoting days were over. We continued to work together in a mutely contracted truce until the job ended. Our supervisor, lacking courage to do his job, had palmed it off on the new kid. I used this lesson in later years to address problems before they became full-blown, and *never* to unload personnel problems on subordinates.

Over the next few years, I saw Ed occasionally at the golf course clubhouse, where we exchanged cool greetings. I did not dream the day would come when I privately acknowledged a debt of silent gratitude to him for the opportunity to hone skills that would later prove invaluable to me. He had helped me in a way that placed him second only to Clarice in my appreciation of people responsible for the most valuable lessons I learned on my first job. In Ed's case, he had simply unwittingly provided me with a foundation of daily shorthand practice that few young people experienced directly on the heels of their formal training. It continues to serve me well to this day.

Part 3

A Tempting Offer

Time Out

The short duration of the OPS job coincided conveniently with the birth of our son, Hartley Jr. in 1953. I was happy to leave the job behind, enjoyed my life at home, and viewed my future as wife and mother with pleasure. In my opinion, the working world couldn't compare to that of home and children. In 1956 our daughter Dawn joined the family. Hartley and I

Donna and Hartley Jr., 1953.

agreed that our family was complete, and he was a good father, participating in activities devoted to children: boy scouts, little league coaching, and Sunday school superintendent. I had developed an interest in painting with oils on canvas, and there was time for me to enjoy this hobby. I loved gardening from the time I was a toddler with a handful of seeds, planting one at a time in the places Daddy pointed out in the straight rows he had dug in the freshly turned Western Minnesota earth. While the children played in the yard, I created flower gardens and invited their help in the hope they would try their hand at gardening someday. I continued favorite pursuits of my earlier life; reading, writing poems and stories, and playing my piano—incorporating these interests into activities with my children.

Hartley was supportive of my need for time to myself, as he expected the same consideration. He was happy to care for the kids in the evening if I wanted to pick up books at the library or go out for a game of bridge with my friends. The couples we socialized with shared our interests outside the roles of parenting. They raised their children as we did, to understand that, like them, we needed time with our friends. Although we knew that parenting was a full-time job it didn't stop us from being individuals and, therefore, I didn't find it necessary to seek fulfillment outside of my home.

Donna with Dawn on Lake Superior, 1958.

Hartley Jr. and Dawn in a traditional Christmas photo atop Wahl's Department Store reindeer, 1957.

I was puzzled by other acquaintances who found their roles as wives and mothers tedious, and gave me the impression that they expected me to express the same restless discontent. As we moved into the 1960s, many women I knew were either going back to work or returning to college, finishing educations interrupted by marriage and children. We had all been raised in a generation overshadowed by economic depression, followed by years of war, but that commonality did not manifest itself uniformly in individual women.

I found myself on the defensive when confronted by questions from working mothers who wanted to know why I continued to exercise my stay-at-home choice. Somehow, I began to feel remiss for not contributing to the family coffers by going out to work in addition to caring for home and children. In that era, "Oh, I'm *just* a housewife," became the stock answer by non-working women in response to the question, "And what do you do?" That answer had an apologetic note that raised my hackles.

On the other hand, professional women also received queries that were demeaning. I recently heard an example of this from a friend who, at a gathering with mostly male colleagues, was asked, "And what does *your* husband do?" implying that any women present in the group had to be defined by their *husband's* profession; it was inconceivable that they could be among the professionals. In other instances, people being presented to professional women and their male assistants, invariably ignored the woman and automatically put out a hand to the assistant, assuming he was in charge, and she was the subordinate.

During those years as a new mother, I received multiple requests to serve in children's activities at school and church, as well as community solicitations for various charitable funds. My suggestions that perhaps we could spread the volunteer work more equitably were met with replies that most women in the community were gainfully employed, thus the gap in volunteer work needed to be filled by stay-at-home housewives. The implication was not lost on us that women at home were doing nothing significant and this would give us something productive to do.

I found myself taking time from home and family to do volunteer work, and I was tiring of expectations that I should feel obligated to take on more than a fair share, thus defeating my purpose in making family my priority. I avoided offering my opinion to friends who became prickly if (speaking only for myself) I stated my firm belief that my children were benefiting from my being at home during their formative years.

Many of the working mothers I knew were using their supplemental income to buy the latest in appliances, luxury items for their homes, and expensive toys for their kids. They felt good about earning money, and though most of them paid dearly for child care, others had family members who were willing to help out with babysitting. Few women's jobs paid well, and I found it hard to believe there was much left after paying for transportation, wardrobe maintenance, and substituting processed foods for less expensive and more nutritious food prepared from fresh ingredients.

Some friends who had worked, agreed that this had been their experience, and came back home. Others were convinced their kids had become more self-reliant, and the mothers were better parents for not having to spend their days at home with lack of adult companionship and conversation.

Breaking Loose

In 1965, during a visit to my children's elementary school in Lakeside, Eugene Bergman, the Principal asked me to stop by his office. He had been a high school acquaintance, graduating a year ahead of me. He told me the school library had to be closed in the afternoons due to budget cuts, and he was determined to find a way to have it open for kids to use the entire school day. His proposed solution was to find a parent willing to form a committee of volunteers to staff the library afternoons. He asked me if I would consider taking on this task. My passion for reading and belief in the importance of developing children's reading skills nudged me to agree to do it during my kids' school hours. I had read with my children daily from the time they were toddlers, and we were often joined by their neighborhood friends who happened along seeking playmates. The short attention span of some of these kids convinced me that they didn't participate in reading time at home. I saw the school library as an opportunity to encourage reading in their early years.

I began enthusiastically by placing myself on the schedule. I was pleased to find enough mothers who didn't work outside their homes to fill in the other afternoons. The very first week, however, I received last-minute calls from people who just couldn't be there for their scheduled time without so much as an apology or valid excuse for skipping what I considered a commitment. I didn't feel justified in pressing that conviction on people who were not being compensated for their time, so each week I found myself spending more time filling in for defectors.

Disillusioned, I was wondering how I could explain to Eugene that this program wasn't working for me. Then one day, an escape hatch opened when I stopped at our neighborhood bank, and the president invited me to his office for a visit. He wanted me to consider coming to work for him.

Options

Hartley and I had moved our bank accounts from downtown to the new North Shore State Bank when it opened in Lakeside. In the next few years, we became acquainted with Jim, its president, and the other staff members. I wasn't surprised that winter day when Jim began what I thought was casual conversation. "I wondered if you ever consider going back to work. We have two openings coming up here, and I'm sure you're qualified to handle either. You might like one of them," Jim said.

I told him honestly that I had no banking experience. Unabashed, Jim continued. "You could start on a trial basis before you make a decision, so you'd have nothing to lose. I hope you'll consider it, and I know you'll want to run it by Hartley. Why don't you think about it and stop back next week."

"I could at least consider it," I said—not wanting to brush off his offer without even letting him explain it, but as I departed, I was convinced I would turn him down. I was sure a bank was the last place in the world I wanted to work.

After I got home and thought about it, I had second thoughts. A job would put me beyond the reach of people who regularly recruited volunteers. My children were moving into junior high and the bank was three blocks from home; I would never be far from my home and children. Although I thought I had no interest in working with numbers, I had done well in math classes. However, my training seemed disconnected from any except the most rudimentary life application. I mentioned Jim's proposal to Hartley, who predictably offered help and support if the idea held any interest for me. I didn't want to be a mother who continued to cling to children, refusing to loosen my grip as they struggled for independence. It also occurred to me that perhaps there wouldn't be anyone to offer me a job when I decided it was time to give the kids some space.

Finally concluding I would listen to Jim's proposal and consider it carefully, I went back to see him the next week. The bank secretary, who was leaving her job soon, didn't have enough work to keep her occupied full-time in this small new bank. The teller line was slightly overstaffed, so Jim proposed that I could easily manage the secretarial work mornings, and move to the first teller window in the afternoon when it was busier. After the 2:00 p.m. closing, the entire staff stayed until the bank's work balanced for the day.

Home proximity to the bank meant free transportation and child care would not be needed, which helped offset the meager salary. In the back of my mind, I wondered if my decision was a means, not only to brush the community dust from my skirt, but to seek approval by becoming a *productive* woman. I stopped second guessing my motives and agreed to try Jim's plan beginning shortly after the new year. Then I hurried home to bake my family's favorite holiday cookies to get a head start on assuaging twinges of guilt for any future neglect.

I had explained the plan to my children, and they readily agreed to do everything they could to help at home. They had been assigned small chores from early ages and, like most kids, needed reminding to get them done. It would have been easier just to do them myself, but we wanted them to share in caring for the house and yard. Hartley agreed to add grocery shopping and vacuum cleaning to his regular yard maintenance jobs. He insisted on installing a dishwasher which our kitchen had been lacking, against my protests that we didn't need one. I appreciated his effort to cut down on household chores.

Revelations

The first week in January 1967 found me at the secretary's desk of the North Shore State Bank in Lakeside. I spent my mornings on correspondence and filing, and after lunch training for the teller work under the tutelage of Dolores Hartikka, the assistant cashier. As a customer, I had been aware that she held this officer's job and was impressed that our bank was so progressive. I would soon learn just how unusual it was to find a woman working in bank management. Dolores was a credit to the business, and a good, patient teacher. The third officer of the bank was Larry Johnson, who as cashier, was the overseer of bank operations.

My mornings were easy, but the afternoons in the first teller window were challenging. In large banks, teller work is categorized by function assigned to specific tellers (savings, checking accounts, drafts, money orders, or traveler checks). In small banks, these functions are handled by all tellers. Some procedures were not repeated often enough to retain them. It was a challenge and took time to become proficient in every function.

Although I had no trouble with math, the number of elements on our accounting forms made it more difficult than I expected to balance my work at the end of a day during the training period. Dolores patiently worked out each problem and the next day I'd find a new way to mess up the day-end accounting. Larry kept an encouraging eye on the process, saying, "How is it going today, Dolores."

"She's doing better. Today we're only $250.01 off."

I knew they were both anxious for me to achieve the required goal of balancing to the last penny. Finally one Friday afternoon, when Larry asked the usual question, "How's it going, Dolores?" She turned her dazzling smile on him and said brightly, "We're close!"

"*My God*" Dolores!" he said, "Are we going for *close* now?"

I was soon balancing to the penny daily. The afternoons brought more customers, and I had no time to be bored. The first window was the most visible and closest to the door so it was a natural choice for customers to stop at my window if there was no line waiting. I thought it would have made sense to put a new teller farther down the line, but I wasn't going to question management decisions.

Now that I was using math in a practical application, I found I liked working with numbers and money. I had forgotten what it was like to spend most of my day with adults, and I was finding the complimentary approval of managers a welcome change from cries of, "Do we have to have oatmeal? Joey's mom lets him have sugar frosted flakes." My return to the adult world was starting to feel comfortable and I began thinking of broadening my horizons.

As business increased, and we began to offer mortgage loans, it became apparent that we needed a full-time secretary to process the related paper work. Imagining myself endlessly typing multiple-copy forms eight hours a day, conjured up negative reflections of my first job with all those government forms! Yet, I was concerned that seeking a new job would take me farther from home—still, I continued to think about possibilities that might be open in a larger institution. Returning to PTA and collecting for charitable organizations was even less appealing than routine typing. If I stopped working, I would miss this new world I had discovered. A friend who had spent some years in Northern City Bank downtown, encouraged me to talk to the personnel manager to see if they had any suitable openings. She was confident it would be a good place for me, and the prospect seemed worth exploring. I called the personnel office at Northern City, one of the two largest banks in the city, and made an appointment for an interview with the manager.

Doug Lewis and Larry Johnson at North Shore Bank of Commerce, ca. 1968.

PART 4

BANK CAPERS

Bulls and Bears

In midsummer of 1967, I interviewed at Northern City National Bank in the Alworth Building. I was surprised when the first thing Wayne, the personnel manager, mentioned was a test. I wasn't averse to testing, but hadn't expected it was a requirement for a teller's job. I finished the test well before the allotted time was up, a little uneasy thinking maybe I missed something. After viewing the results, Wayne suggested that I would be bored by the available commercial banking jobs, but I might be interested in an unusual opening in the trust department. He described the duties as buying and selling securities for bank customers and maintaining them in safekeeping accounts. It sounded interesting, and I agreed to meet with the investment director.

On the second floor, the ornate elevator doors opened directly into a reception area, where an attractive young woman greeted clients and handled the small switchboard. A partial wall separated the tastefully appointed front offices from the accounting area in back. John, the investment director, a thin greying figure in matching grey suit, greeted me with an old-fashioned courtly manner. His smile of approval convinced me that Wayne had already told John he had found the person they were looking for. We got on well and he wasted no time offering me the job. I would begin two weeks from Monday.

I reported to Wayne's office on my first day to take care of final details of hiring. He escorted me to the second floor to show me around and introduce me to the staff. As I surveyed the spacious office, I noticed that, although the men had handsome brass nameplates on their desks, the women had no identification. I was puzzled that the men had single line phones on their desks; women's desks were devoid of phones.

Wayne began introductions in the investment department where I met Fern, the director's secretary; Fred, the investment officer who would be my immediate supervisor; and Tom, the other investment officer in the group. John came out of his office to welcome me, and we visited with Jan, the young woman I was replacing, about my training. Moving on, he introduced me to the trust officers and managers, but none of their secretaries. This made no sense to me since I would certainly expect to interact with the women as well as the men. Were the women regarded as part of the fixtures? Yet, in days to come I would find, contrary to my initial impression, that the women played a vital role in this fiduciary business. Though not recognized as key staff members by the corporation, we were valued and trusted by our supervisors, but perhaps taken for granted—in the same manner as were most women who worked as homemakers.

The atmosphere was dignified and quiet, except for the clacking of typewriter keys. There were two glassed-in offices for the senior trust officers, and two offices with outside windows facing Superior Street, occupied by Ray, the attorney who headed the trust department, and John, the investment director. The other trust officers and clerical employees worked in a spacious open area with good furniture and an extra chair beside each desk. My desk faced a library of reference books and periodicals, such as Standard and Poors and Moody's periodicals, related to investment and laws governing trust services.

A phone rang on one of the desks, and a secretary sprinted from her desk, lunging to catch it on its third ring. She screened the call, handed the receiver to the man at the desk and returned to her work. The archaic phone system needed upgrading, and I made a mental note to look for an opportunity to do something about changing it.

A door next to the elevators led to the board room where the bank directors met and the trust and investment officers reviewed their administrative work at regular intervals. On the west corner, next to the offices, a smaller conference room was discreetly tucked away next to a private elevator restricted to bank employees, which ran from basement to second floor. It saved time waiting for public elevators and afforded security for transfer of valuable certificates from the main vault in the basement to the trust department.

Trust officers were required to wear white shirts and ties with their suits. They were allowed to remove their jackets when they had no clients at their desks. Clients could smoke; trust officers could smoke only when they had no clients at their desks. Women could not smoke in the office. We dressed in suits or dresses with tasteful accessories, and used discreetly applied makeup. The dress code would change for both men and women during the years I worked there, but it was well before the days of "casual Fridays." Casual dress for us meant colored shirts for men and pants suits for women. Although an overall climate of formality prevailed, everyone was on a first-name basis.

When I began to work with Jan, I discovered she worked by rote and eyed me curiously before she dismissed a number of my questions by saying, "You don't need to know that; it doesn't matter." What a strange response I thought, but after a few of these exchanges, I realized she didn't know the answers and couldn't fathom why I wanted more information than she could provide. I stopped asking questions and took notes; I could dig out the answers for myself later. Jan was friendly, but I was relieved when she left and I could start learning. Fred was already taking life easy in anticipation of his impending retirement in Arizona. He handled the major trading of stocks and bonds for the trust department, and was an astute investment advisor. It was to his advantage to answer my questions, as it paved the way for him to assign more of his work to me than he had delegated to my predecessor. Although I learned a lot from Fred, neither of us were authorized to offer investment advice to my clients, whose portfolios I held in safekeeping. Our service was restricted to explaining various investments, current prices, and yields. Investment consultation was offered only to trust account clients.

As computer technology advanced, the practice of issuing stock and bond certificates, or registering them in the clients' names gradually became obsolete, thus eliminating time-consuming manual transfer of stock shares or bond certificates. Accounts were recorded on computer printouts rather than bulky folders of certificates in the bank vault.

My greatest concern about working downtown had been that one of my children would need attention for an illness or injury, and I wouldn't be there for them. The fact was that parents who don't work are not always at home on a moment's notice, but that was little comfort to me. As the cold weather set in, I didn't have long to wait before Dawn had to be home a few days with an ear infection. I was fraught with guilt feelings, even though a friend and neighbor looked in on her and took care of her medication and lunch, and she recovered quickly.

The next experience was quite different. One day in mid-morning I received a call at work from the principal at Ordean Junior High, who informed me tersely that Hartley Jr. had injured his foot in gym class and I should get right to the school office to pick him up and take him to the clinic for x-rays. I reminded him that I was downtown, and it would take me a little time to get there.

"Well, get here as quickly as you can. We are not responsible for getting students to medical facilities."

I explained to my boss that I would have to leave for perhaps the rest of the morning. I did not have a car, and while I was trying to think how to manage the problem, my boss was saying to one of the officers, "Lee, can you go with Donna to Ordean? I have a bank car waiting downstairs. Her son has an injured foot and we need to get him to the clinic in Lakeside. I don't think she should go alone."

With no hesitation, Lee said, "I can leave right now. Come on, Donna. Let's go!"

As we left, Fred called out, "I'll take care of your transactions if you can't get back today."

On the ride down East Superior Street, I thought about

how much easier it had been to handle this from work than it would have been alone from my home in Lakeside only six blocks from the school. We pulled up in front of Ordean, Lee walked into the office, swooped Hartley up, and carried him out, as I introduced the tall trust officer to the startled principal. Hartley had his x-ray, nothing was broken, and we had him settled comfortably at home well before noon.

Harbingers of Change

I was becoming comfortable in my job when new trends made inroads into the banking business in larger cities, and would soon affect our environment. Locally owned banks being absorbed by large corporations, were subject to operate under management guidelines set forth by corporate headquarters. The president of our commercial bank operation was not a native of our city unlike most of our other officers—he had moved to Duluth from a western state where he worked for the First Bank Corporation, which would take over our bank just months after my job began.

There was speculation that management would change drastically, but the changes were subtle at first. It was common knowledge that the corporation wanted to consolidate the entire bank under the control of the commercial bank president. Ray, the attorney who headed the trust department, was adamant that we keep the status quo, with the trust department operating as a separate entity. It was hard to argue with his success in managing the trust business, which evidently gave him enough clout to maintain control for the time being, and we continued to work under his leadership.

Then one Saturday, after a round of golf at Northland Country Club, Ray was stricken with a fatal heart attack. Ray had held his position for many years and was respected by everyone in the department. It was the end of an era in our institution, and we had no idea how deeply this loss would affect our working lives.

53

After much procrastination, the bank directors announced that our two senior trust officers, Les and Charles would share Ray's place and, since neither of them had a law degree, a new attorney would be hired. This division of power was the perfect strategy to set the stage for consolidation of trust services with the commercial bank. It didn't change overnight—it came by degrees. The department Ray so carefully protected lost some of its luster and proud spirit. Noel, an attorney from Minneapolis, was installed in Ray's office and Les and Charles remained in their old offices. Noel was a good choice and remained in his position until after I left several years later. The new arrangement didn't affect the investment department—John continued to lead our group, Fred remained as my immediate supervisor and it seemed like business as usual.

Fred's duties included administering guardianship accounts—legal arrangements between banks and courts to administer funds of people who had been declared incompetent. The accounts were divided between trust departments of the larger banks in the city with a small fee paid by the court. Although the bank was not named guardian of the person (only their money) the clients came to their trust officers seeking help for their life problems. It was an incongruous aspect of trust work where the client pool represented a small melting pot of sorts. Many of our trust clients were wealthy, as were some of the guardianship clients. Others were endowed with small pensions, linked to the others in their group only by the common denominator of having been declared unable to manage their money. In this part of Fred's job he displayed a compassionate side to his character. He was unfailingly attentive to all of these clients, listening to their troubles with the patience of a kindly father, endearing him to clients and fellow workers alike.

When John summoned me to his office one day after my first few months of employment, I didn't consider it a good sign. I was pleasantly surprised, however, by his opening line, "I'm raising your salary. You're earning far too little for the work you're doing. I don't hold with the idea that men should be better paid than women who are capable of handling the same work. I see how much you've learned, and your work is appreciated." John had treated me with consideration from the day I started my job. His outward appearance and demeanor, which suggested a throwback to the Victorian era, concealed an astute, forward-thinking man of business. He mentioned my rapid grasp of investment and trust functions and liked my work with the investment customers. He went on to say, "I have an idea that might interest you. I have been thinking for some time of introducing a new job in our department. We need a women's representative to offer consultation for beneficiaries of trust accounts, as well as the customers you already help with investments. Usually our beneficiaries are widows, who often resent having yet another man managing their money."

"It's brilliant, John. Most men don't understand that our women beneficiaries have managed households and are not helpless." It was a natural, and my enthusiasm gained momentum as I continued, "I agree with your idea completely. Long-range, it might not be needed indefinitely, but it could be an important transition to open the door for women's participation in managing their own or family assets. Their husbands want to spare them from financial concerns, and they haven't had a chance to handle money except for household allowances. They do need some guidance, and I think they'd accept it better from a woman than a male trust officer. Another advantage is that your plan would save trust officers' time they could apply to account reviews."

Thoughts were tumbling one after another in my head, remembering unhappy clients coming to me with concerns and questions, feeling men had treated them like little girls who shouldn't have to trouble their *pretty heads* over finances. John's idea was timely, with the potential of building a bridge for women to participate actively in family financial management.

John had resumed speaking, "Would you be interested in the job? I believe you are the best qualified woman we have to fill the position. Of course we'd need to provide you with clerical help."

I quickly agreed that I would love to take on the job, but the timing of John's proposal was unfortunate with our bank now a part of a large corporation. That was when I really began to feel the restrictions of the new regime. There was no provision in the corporate budget for mollycoddling women customers. John's vision didn't stand a chance, however it encouraged me to know there were men who had the foresight to recognize the changing times. John had the ability to translate his convictions for his colleagues who focused on their fear that women would find a chink to break into their domain, and he would be followed by other men who shared his foresight. I was impressed by this unusual man's attention to the effort made by the people he hired and, when warranted, his effort to help them realize their potential.

Painful Transition

As we moved through the 1960s, typewriters displayed new faces, and photocopiers were replacing carbon copies so successfully that copies of legal documents had to be stamped PHOTOCOPY to distinguish them from the originals.

Performance reviews of clerical employees were primarily based on speed and accuracy of their work, consequently this became the yardstick by which they judged their own value. They had each developed speed and skill on their own typewriter (most of them electric by the '60s) and they were reluctant to adapt their skills to new models, fearing the transition would lower speed and efficiency—their stock in trade. This made it easy for supervisors, who authorized new equipment acquisitions from their department budgets, to pass over new models touted by purveyors of office products.

But when updated equipment appeared in one department, it became a matter of prestige, and workers in adjacent departments were quickly aware of their neighbors' new equipment. Torn between adjusting to strange new machines or being left behind, they gave in to progress. Soon their department received regular visits from service people to repair mysterious maladies that began plaguing their typewriters, thus reminding their department head that they were still using obsolete junk.

In 1967, when I began working in the Northern City investment department, the typewriters used by the secretaries had all recently been replaced by new IBM Electric models of their choice. My investment work required minimal typing and my desk was equipped with a Smith-Corona manual typewriter. It was very much like the machines I used in school to learn typing, and was perfectly adequate for the bits and pieces I needed to type.

I had been there a few months when the office manager declared my typewriter due for replacement and asked me what make and model I would like. I suggested an IBM Selectric II, an innovative model which had entered the market in 1961. I had used one on my previous job and liked it. The alphabet was arranged on a round element that moved back and forth with a ribbon cartridge. There were no flying keys clattering and jamming and no platen or carriage to return at the ding of a bell. It stored information electronically and "caught up" after the typist stopped striking keys. An added feature allowed the user to change fonts by removing the element and replacing it with another style of type.

The next morning, Jack the IBM sales rep, delivered the Selectric II. When the strange, slick machine was placed on my desk, the secretaries were wide-eyed, but not happy. I had worked harmoniously with them and was surprised to be assailed by almost hostile questions and comments, "Why didn't you order the same model we have?" "We're supposed to all use the same equipment." "You won't like it—I hear they are slow. You won't be able to type as fast." "Did you *ask* for that model?"

I admitted I had been given a choice and this was it. Since I had a different job than the secretaries, I didn't think it mattered if my typewriter was a different model. I explained it seemed slow because there were no keys flying and no carriage being shifted. I didn't want to alienate my workmates, who were clustered around my desk like a flock of chickens in a henhouse, ready to move in for the attack on one of their brood who appeared to be wounded. I invited them to try the Selectric, but they all rejected this friendly overture with comments like, "I wouldn't touch that thing with a ten-foot pole!" At least I didn't get the silent treatment. They contented themselves with eying my new beauty scornfully to express their disapproval. About a week later, I returned from lunch to find Marlis, the secretary to the trust department head sitting at my desk tentatively hitting a few keys of the Selecric. I picked up a letter from my desk and suggested she copy it. She began typing, but commented, "It seems to hesitate and stall so I have to stop typing."

"Just keep striking keys; the words are being stored, and it will continue to print after you stop typing." Their interest piqued, other secretaries appeared at my desk and, following the leader, they all tried it out. I demonstrated changing the font by replacing the element with another style of type, and they grudgingly admitted it seemed *nice*.

The classic IBM Selectric typewriter and its unique type ball.

I wasn't surprised when the IBM service person began making regular appearances to take care of "problems" with the almost new typewriters. There was even a mishap of spilled *Wite Out* corrective fluid in the interior of one typewriter, rendering the machine useless. The department head got the message and within the month, new Selectrics adorned the desks of every secretary. The IBM salesperson was delighted with the large order, and our entire department was delighted with the dramatic drop in the department's noise level.

The Selectric represented the last major innovation in typewriters. It was the first choice of typists until the introduction of word processors, just a heartbeat before personal computers brought an irrevocable change to office communications.

On Promoting Efficiency

Following the absorption of Northern City by First Bank System, a team of efficiency experts arrived to study the use of employees' time throughout the bank. We were required to log every task we accomplished, and account for every minute away from our desks, including trips to the restrooms. After our indignation subsided, it became a joke among the employees and we simply put up with it until the specialists went away. As a parting salvo, one officer had added a new category to the "official" survey, which he headed, "Time Spent Recording Time Spent." No conclusions emerged, and when the efficiency experts left, it was back to business as usual. When Fred made a scornful remark about the waste of time the time study had been I said, "I'm surprised they didn't recommend revision of the outmoded phone system. It seems they overlooked the most obvious waste of secretaries' time sprinting around to answer phones throughout the department." Fred bristled, "What do you mean?"

"Well, the secretaries answer the phones, but they have

to run all over the office to do it. Why don't they have phones at their desks with access to the lines they need to answer? It's inefficient—a waste of time and energy."

"Oh that," Fred said with a dismissive wave of his hand. "We can't let women have telephones; we'd never get any work out of them. They'd be making personal calls all day."

I couldn't resist his jibe, "Fred, your chauvinistic comment is about as enlightened as the bad Bob Hope joke of the 1940s, when he claimed there were three methods of communication: telephone, telegraph, and tell-a-woman." This elicited a hearty laugh, but our conversation did not inspire him to seek a resolution to the phone problem. An opportunity soon arose for me to introduce the subject when Lee, the office manager confided to me that he had recently been given carte blanche to redecorate the entire trust department. "Really? Does that include the archaic phone system? I wonder if the department heads share Fred's notion that women can't be trusted with telephones on their desks."

Lee's response to this question was as nonplussed as Fred's had been, "What are you talking about?" I explained my observations about the phone system and suggested that the office remodeling offered the ideal opportunity for a revision.

"Could you create a plan to efficiently cover the whole department's telephone needs?" Since he had no experience with this aspect of office setup, he was happy to turn it over to me.

I agreed to prepare a layout of the entire second floor with my recommendations. Was I an expert in this field? No, but I knew one. I consulted my sister Wanda, who was a manager at Northwestern Bell. She showed me the available systems and we sketched out a plan.

Lee's only concern when he viewed it was my recommendation to stagger coffee breaks and lunch hours to ensure efficient coverage. "I don't think the secretaries will like this. They're used to going together for breaks."

I assured him I'd talk to the secretaries. I suggested that

the scheduling might offer them an opportunity to become better acquainted with employees in other departments. They understood that this wasn't high school, but a business office, as I knew they would, and they liked the tradeoff for the convenience of multiple phone lines, accessible from their own desks.

My coworkers were aware of my interest in art and knew I painted in oils, so when the renovation of the department was complete, Lee told me the management staff had asked if I would be willing to select artwork to hang on the newly painted walls. I was intrigued by the opportunity to search for the right pieces for a combination of work by local artists and older works newly available for sale. I invited another woman to accompany me for a second opinion, and we visited studios and galleries until we had assembled a collection of original art. Surprisingly, I was given no budget figure, and simply chose by using my own judgment. I didn't consider it an addition to my resumé, but on the other hand, I found it didn't hurt my image with management.

High Jinx

Fred had worked at the bank all his adult life, and this long history was revealed to me on my first day when he said with some pride, "You know the people in the commercial bank call the trust department *the silk stocking crowd*." The last time I had heard any mention of silk stockings was before WWII, but Fred still considered the label a symbol of elite status; it was part of his charm. He was loved by most people for that charm and propensity for unrestrained practical joking.

Many years earlier, when it was time for his boss to retire, Fred considered himself the heir apparent, the logical choice to take over his job. According to bank lore, his promotion was thwarted by his own casual, jokey attitude, and John was hired for the job. Fred was less than objective about being overlooked and focused the blame on John, who became his new boss. Fred could not forget the past, and continued to express his resentment in petty ways.

He liked to arrive at work early to pick up the just-delivered *Wall Street Journal* from the front desk before the receptionist brought the paper to John's office. Fred then took the paper to his desk for a ritual clipping of carefully selected articles, and when it was tattered to his satisfaction, he carefully refolded it and placed it on John's desk. He surreptitiously watched John open the riddled journal, hoping for a reaction that was never forthcoming. John simply went out and picked up a copy from another area of the bank, returned to his office and began to read.

Although everyone (including John) knew who perpetrated this desecration of the investor's bible, not a word or snicker was uttered. They were in silent agreement that Fred was incorrigible, but knew the problem would soon resolve itself when he retired. Yet, it disrupted the work of others, and I wondered how he was approaching the end of his working days without having realized the joke had been over for years.

Like most companies the bank practiced the ritual of an annual holiday party each December. Our party, which was anticipated for weeks ahead, was held at the Hotel Duluth ballroom. It was a lavish affair, including all employees in the commercial bank and the trust department. I had served on the planning committee from my first year at the bank. Our arrangements started with booking a musical group for the entertainment segment and an orchestra for after dinner dancing. There were no budget restrictions; expenditures were at the discretion of the committee members who unanimously agreed that the planning was as much fun as the party. We exercised our creativity in writing skits including a few wicked parodies featuring eccentricities of managers. By mutual consent we left our best material on the cutting room floor in the interest of job security. The cocktail hour and gourmet dinner were restricted to employees; spouses and guests of employees were welcome to join the party for the dance that followed where, to discourage overindulgence in cocktails, there was a cash bar.

Every employee received a tasteful gift selected from

the treasures at Bagley's Jewelry store, which were distributed by Santa Claus who arrived after dinner. Due to the number of employees, distribution was a time-consuming business, so one year to speed it up I designed a costume for an elf to assist in the presentations. I coerced Dennis, a tall, lanky, bespectacled loan officer to don the green felt outfit and take on the elf role. No one knew of this new addition until Santa arrived and Dennis skipped in behind him with bells tinkling on the turned-up toes of his green felt slippers and the peak of his jaunty matching hat. He was a rousing success, and the elf became an annual feature of Santa's ritual.

Each year, a new candidate was selected, and each year I had to design a new outfit because the elf costume mysteriously disappeared. I decided it was small reward for the performance, and since banker elves came in all shapes and sizes, they needed made-to-order garb. I became an adept designer of elf apparel and as each holiday season neared, there was much speculation about who would skip in behind Santa to hoots of laughter and wild applause. I had numerous willing candidates, but my selection was a well-guarded secret. It seemed odd that such a silly caper caught on with this group of staid bankers.

We could expect a few people to get a little out of line each year after partaking of the free cocktail hour libations. One year, the festivities were interrupted when an exuberant bank officer, weary of the president's overlong after-dinner speech, fired a baked potato at him across the dining room, shouting, "Sit down and shut up!" The president laughingly dodged the flying spud and judiciously sat down. We thought we might be short one popular officer the next day, but there were no obvious repercussions.

One incident became legend in the annals of Christmas party stories. It involved Fred, who needed a ride to the first holiday party I attended. He lived in my neighborhood, so I offered to pick him up. Hartley volunteered to drive us to the hotel, drop us off at the lobby and come back for us after the party. On our way to the hotel, Fred told us the amazing tale of why he couldn't drive his car to the party. Many years earlier, he and two fellow bankers had overindulged at the free bar during the evening, and decided to stop at the Coney Island on First Street for a hot dogs before driving home. Fred had parked near the Coney Island, so they set out on foot. After their repast, they were weaving down First Street to retrieve Fred's car when a police squad approached. An officer got out and asked, "Are you planning to drive that car?"

Fred admitted they were. "You aren't in any condition to drive. Leave it where it is and take a cab."

When they solemnly assured him they would take a cab, the squad car continued on its rounds. Looking around for a cab, Fred spotted one in front of a bar where the driver had gone inside to locate his fare. The motor was running and, ostensibly following the police officer's admonition, they took the cab.

Feeling very responsible, Fred dropped his friends off, drove home, and parked the cab in his driveway. When daylight came and his wife asked what a cab was doing in their driveway, there was hell to pay. Somehow he managed to avoid formal charges or publicity, but he was never allowed to drive to the Christmas party again, and the story followed him until the day he retired.

Corporate sponsored gatherings became less prevalent among employers in the 1970s and 1980s. I sometimes wonder if the spirit of camaraderie that prevailed at our celebrations still exists in today's business organizations.

Gender Gap

Progress in technology was only one element subject to change in the 1960s and 1970s. Betty Friedan's book *The Feminine Mystique*, shook women to their foundations like an earthquake, with aftershocks felt around the world. The resulting tsunami brought forth a number of feminist leaders who mobilized groups (many of them comprised of single mothers) to protest the discrepancies in pay, benefits, and working conditions between men and women. As their cause gained momentum through the sixties, some became militant scorning feminine dress and assuming strident voices.

In the midst of the developing splinter groups, along came Gloria Steinem, beautiful and intelligent, her strong but well-modulated voice exuding confidence. She became a persuasive leader of the cause. In a time of mixed messages and confusion for both men and women, making navigation of troubled waters difficult, she tirelessly lead the way to turn the tide for working women across the country.

New York Times columnist, Gail Collins in her book, *When Everything Changed (the amazing journey of American Women from 1960 to the present)* published by Little Brown and Company in 2009, chronicles these struggles seeking equal rights for women, and in-depth stories of the many leaders who participated.

In 1977, I was particularly aware of one early attempt to gain employment equality involving banking, which hit close to home. Eight women tellers at the Citizens National Bank in the small town of Willmar, Minnesota, conducted one of the first gender-discrimination strikes. The women had endured years of low pay with no chance for promotion, though clearly qualified. The bank manager expected the female tellers to train a young man hired for a non-posted position as a loan officer. It was too much; they decided to strike. They donned snowmobile suits and began their march with homemade signs in wind chills that reached minus seventy degrees. Hoping for a new contract, they walked their walk for over a year to no avail. They received meager support from the community, and the lawyer who represented them fared no better. He soon lost his seat as a county chairperson for the Republication party. Their story was picked up by news services and published in newspapers around the country. Some of the tellers appeared on television talk shows.

The National Labor Relations Board ultimately ruled that labor practices had not caused the strike. The only one of the eight who went back to work was demoted. The others were unable to find new jobs. Yet, they had captured the attention of the nation, and became one of the groups who broke ground for better opportunities for women in banking. In 1981, Lee Grant was inspired to produce a documentary filmed on site including interviews with the eight women, labor leaders, and townspeople. It was the largest strike against a bank in American history.

A decade earlier when I began my years in banking, I recalled how pleased I was to find a woman officer in our small neighborhood North Shore Bank of Commerce, imagining it was step forward in banking. I realized later how naive I had been. It was many years before I saw another female officer in any other bank.

A Time to Move On

The time came for Fred to retire, which raised the question of how to distribute his work. It was obvious that I was doing much of it, and I was invited to the office of the president to discuss my future. The decision had been made to move my job from the trust department to the commercial bank on the first floor. I would not be responsible for any of Fred's trust investment purchases or guardianship accounts. The president offered me a modest pay raise to assume sole responsibility for customer investment transactions and their safekeeping accounts. My job would continue to be categorized as "investment clerk." I objected to both the salary and the lack of acknowledgement for the work I had been doing with no direction from my designated supervisor.

One of the elements of change that had occurred in the years I worked in the investment business was the increasing number of small investors who were replacing their savings accounts and bank certificates with U.S. Treasury bills, notes and bonds, now issued in smaller denominations than had previously been offered. Syndicated investment columnists, such as Sylvia Porter, encouraged small investors to move their savings into these higher yield securities. They were backed by the full faith and credit of the U.S. Treasury so they had the additional attraction of safety. The good news, which increased the public's buying frenzy, was that local banks handled these transactions without a service charge. I pointed out that this had increased the number of my safekeeping accounts to the point where I needed clerical help to finish my daily paperwork by the end of banking business at 2:00 p.m.

The solution offered by the president was, "You'll have a supervisor. Bill will initial all your transactions, so you won't really be responsible, and any of the loan officers can talk to your customers about investment. They wouldn't be working here if they didn't understand the investment business. That will give you enough time to take care of the extra paperwork." Then, spreading the icing on the cake, he said with a kind of smirk, "You know we can't give the responsibility for a job like this to a woman—you ladies run off on us to have babies."

At this juncture, I couldn't hold back. "You mean like the marketing manager who was here only a month before he ran off on you when someone made him a better offer?" I must give the president credit for evading that acerbic observation as adroitly as he dodged the baked potato lobbed at him during the Christmas party. I wasn't quite ready to throw away the years of work I had invested in a job I liked, so I continued our discussion: "I have doubts that your loan officers are qualified to answer customer questions related to their investment needs. It is unlikely they all keep up on current prices and yields of even U. S. Treasury offerings."

He responded to this by inviting me to the Monday morning staff meeting of the bank officers—the first woman to experience that dubious honor. He was certain that they would put my mind at ease regarding their willingness and ability to take on customer calls by phone or in person. In the presence of their boss, the gentlemen were attentive, feigned interest, and asked questions, but I was convinced they would never be available when a customer showed up with questions. This was quickly verified, and even Bill, my designated supervisor declared arrogantly when I expected him to participate in a customer transaction, "If you think I'm going to monkey with that junk, you're crazy!"

Later, he finally offered part-time help of one of the executive secretaries, to assist with the overload this new business represented, but an hour of her time here and there fell woefully short of the help I needed. The shiny new nameplate on my desk did not mollify me.

I was taking care of all customer contacts; it was no surprise to me that the bank officers made themselves unavailable to assist me as I had been assured they would. I acknowledged to myself that this job which showed no credit on the bottom line of the bank's balance sheet was considered a liability by this big shortsighted corporation. I did not take it personally, but decided it was time to move on, and so turned in my resignation. A subsequent discussion with Wayne (that management like to call an "exit interview") did not convince me that anything would be changed to my satisfaction. His assurances that we could "work something out," that women would soon be recognized for their contributions, fell on cynical ears. I simply said, "Wayne, I have heard it all before. There has been ample time to respond to my concerns in the months they have been ignored."

Knowing I would not reconsider he told me of a conversation he had had with the president. When Wayne explained to the him that my job was not simply a clerical function, he responded with an assurance that my replacement would handle the job with no problem. Wayne said he didn't think I'd reconsider, which the president dismissed by saying, "Don't worry—in six months we'll have forgotten she ever worked here."

Wayne had done his best, and I was sorry he would have

to struggle keeping anyone in that job. Before I left his office, I thanked him for the efforts he had made on behalf of me and other women employees. The president was not in the bank on my last day, but the following day, I received an overblown letter from him complimenting me on my fine contribution and apologizing that he couldn't be there on my last day to speak to me in person.

About six weeks after I left, a friend from the mortgage department called me to say that my replacement had quit a few weeks after I left. I was amused, but not surprised. My replacement was older and wiser than I, and I knew if she didn't get the necessary help, she wouldn't waste time struggling with it. My friend told me that she had been reassigned to take over the job with two other people assisting her with the overload. She thought I deserved to know. I also learned that now all women in the bank had shiny new nameplates on their desks. If they hadn't "arrived," at least they had identities.

Twenty-five years later, former employees of the bank got together every few years for reunions with those who had worked together, along with current employees.

Northern City Bank Trust Officers Tom Gronlund and Don Nygaard, ca. 1990.

Donna and Trust
Director Les Shervy
with his Secretary
Ann Mattson,
ca. 1990.

That was before personal computers and the disappearance of regulations changed the face of banking irrevocably. Hartley and I were seated at a table with Les and his wife when the former president asked if he and his wife could join us. I almost felt sorry for him as he fumbled with words trying to apologize for the unfairness of my treatment all those years ago, saying, "It was the times; some things couldn't be helped." I appreciated that he had the courage to address the issue, but simply said, "It was a long time ago."

Hartley and I just exchanged knowing looks and smiled. By then we were running a successful business of our own—treating our employees the way I would have liked to be treated.

Interlude

After leaving the bank, I accepted a well-paying job in my field at a downtown office where a small staff managed the assets of a respected local family. I interviewed with the manager who gave an exaggerated job description that focused on the job's most appealing aspects to the point that the reality didn't come close my expectations. When this had occurred in the past, I stayed only long enough to assess these "interim placements" fairly before giving my two-week notice and leaving without a qualm. I include this story here to illustrate its usefulness as a learning experience.

Mary, who had held the job for some years before this time, was a casual acquaintance approaching middle age, intelligent, and pleasant. Although I enjoyed visiting with her, we never discussed our work which was confidential in nature. We had had no conversation about her plans to move from Duluth before I interviewed for her job. I learned from mutual acquaintances that Mary had left the city following a whirlwind courtship and subsequent marriage.

If Mr. Clark, the office manager, had given me an accurate description of this deceptively well-paying position, I would not have agreed to replace her. He characterized the work as challenging and interesting, claiming it was well suited to my qualifications. I was shocked and dismayed as I began my new job and realized what a distorted picture of the *challenging work* he had presented to me. In addition, while he was pleasant and smiling during our interview, in the office he proved to be an overbearing taskmaster, whose surly management style created a toxic work atmosphere. The exception was during visits by the owner and clients when he assumed a Uriah Heep persona, smiling, simpering, and with a dip of his chin, executing little half-bows in their direction. Dickens, however, portrayed Heep in David Copperfield as cadaverous, unlike this almost rotund man, who more closely resembled Shakespeare's description of the justice in *As You Like It* (*The Seven Ages of Man*) "...in fair round belly with good capon lined, with eyes severe..."

The other inhabitants who shared the office were a male accountant and a woman who presumably handled the "challenging and interesting" duties described in my interview. We were treated like chattel; Mr Clark avoided eye contact with the office staff—assignments were meted out with a few brief barks of instruction. Although they were both ideal working companions, the others said little beyond "business talk" and a quiet "good morning" like people do in church. We called the manager "Mr. Clark," and he called us by our first names. I was sorely tempted to inform him that I preferred "Ms. Schilling" to "Donna," but since I already knew I would be leaving it was not worth the trouble.

My biggest challenge was staying awake to plod through the tedious days of routine form typing that had been generated by computer in my previous job. I stuck it out two months before I respectfully gave my notice, truthfully explaining to Mr. Clark that the job did not meet my expectations. He responded angrily, "I was planning to let you go for incompetence anyway—but if you insist on leaving, you won't get a letter of recommendation—you won't get another job in this town."

I was incredulous. Why would he exert pressure on me to stay if I was really incompetent? I did a slow burn, but laughed aloud. Then I said quietly. "We'll see about that."

Without another word, I walked a block down Superior Street to the office of the family's attorney, who was Mr. Clark's direct supervisor. We had become acquainted during my years in investment work, and I knew him to be a man of integrity. I told the receptionist that I needed to speak to him immediately. She showed me to his office door where he greeted me cordially.

I was certain he didn't know how Mr. Clark treated employees so, without preamble, I began our conversation with, "You know me, and you're familiar with my work. I'm sorry I find it necessary to tell you that your manager misrepresented my job when he hired me—I gave my notice, and he threatened that if I leave, he will claim he fired me for incompetence and refuse to provide any references. I know this isn't the way you do business."

"I'm sorry about this—any time you want a reference, let me know and I'll take care of it personally. I was pleased when you came to work for us, but puzzled that you accepted a job of such narrow scope. Now I understand." He thanked me for coming to him with a problem that needed his attention, and assured me he would see to it promptly.

After leaving the job, I was surprised to receive a phone call from Mary who had learned of my hiring and prompt resignation. She was apologetic that there had been no opportunity for her to warn me. "You were wise in leaving before tax season. That was when I really wanted to cut and run," Mary said with a chuckle.

I was thinking I had wasted time and energy by judging job quality by the salary and readily accepting Mr. Clark's glowing description. On the positive side, I had learned how important it is to regard interviews as search for a placement suitable and satisfying to both employer and applicant. This point of view proved to benefit not only me, but people I would soon be hiring.

PART 5

SNOW BUSINESS

23 Skidoo

As a youngster, I overheard an adult use the phrase 23 Skidoo. Puzzled, I asked Mother what it meant and was surprised at her unhesitating answer, "It means skedaddle." We all knew what skedaddle meant—when we were underfoot, Mother often said, "You kids skedaddle outside and play." Her voice took on a wistful note as she expanded on her answer to my question by explaining, "It's a saying from the *Roaring Twenties* when I was young, before the depression."

As years went on I heard and read many other references to the twenties as "the good old days"—flappers living in the fast lane and always dashing off somewhere with great eclat, bathtub gin, and rumble seats of Model A Fords—those days before the stock market crash of 1929.

In researching the *23 Skidoo* phrase to verify the source, I found Mother's definition of "skedaddle" in keeping with that of my dictionary, which defined it: "as to depart hastily, flee." The twenty-three was more difficult to pin down. The internet, listed several origins, but the story I liked best was related to the New York location of the Flatiron Building built in 1902 at Madison Square on Fifth Avenue and Twenty-third Street.

On windy days, the Flatiron's triangular configuration and juxtaposition with neighboring structures created a wind tunnel that caused gusts to swirl around the Flatiron, blowing up women's skirts to show a shapely leg. In windy weather, a number of men hung around the front of the building hoping for a glimpse of a feminine calf (or even a thigh.) Constables allegedly sent them packing by shouting, "23 Skidoo!" Twenty-three referred to the street number. A cartoon from 1906

WELL I'LL BE BLOWED

depicts the scene on a windy day with the Flatiron in the background. This was the most prevalent story of the phrase picked up by New Yorkers and soon spread across the country to become a favorite slang phrase of the *Roaring Twenties.*

I hadn't thought of the breezy phrase for many years when, in the 1960s, we began hearing about a new recreational vehicle, the first snowmobile, created by a Canadian manufacturer of forestry products, Bombardier, Ltd. The motorized sled which "skedaddled" over the snow was tagged with the imaginative trade name of *Ski-Doo*—undeniably perfect for this bright yellow winter toy. It carried an air of panache reminiscent of the carefree days that Mother described. To this day, it remains my favorite adaptation of a catch-phrase for product identification.

I was well over thirty when I had my first snowmobile ride clinging precariously to the back of an early Elan model *Ski-Doo* with my nephew at the helm, careening along a wooded trail in the pale moonlight, the whine of the engine disturbing forest creatures in their habitat, and branches from low-growing underbrush clutching at our clothing. I decided I probably would have loved it fifteen years earlier. The last thing I could have imagined was working for Bombardier, but in 1974, I interviewed with Jerry Calengor for a job in his department of that corporation. Jerry had just been named sales manager of Bombardier, newly reorganized to become the American Distributor of *Ski-Doo* snowmobiles, *Can-Am* Motorcycles, and related clothing and accessories. During our interview, Jerry who was known to the staff as JC, explained to me that several independent distributors were consolidated to create the new corporation. Duluth had been the home base for Halvorson, the largest of those distributors, and many of their managers and employees formed the nucleus of Bombardier Corporation, which remained in Duluth.

*Ski-Doo*s and other products transported from the factory in Montreal were shipped throughout the United States via Halvor Lines, a trucking company created by Roy Halvorson. Halvor continued to ship the product for the new corporation. Several other sales supporting departments were housed in the Duluth facility; shipping, marketing, accounting, service, warranty, parts, and data processing.

JC faced the challenge of reorganizing the consolidated distributors' territories, adding to his sales force and keeping support departments informed of changes. The changeover had to be done without a pause in the daily business of sales and deliveries. He had decided he needed to take time for interviewing and selecting his own secretary to assist with the challenge, and he offered me the job. He didn't minimize the task ahead of us explaining that it would be a ground-breaking effort. I liked his honesty, and I believed we'd work well together.

"Our two top priorities have to be creating a line of communication with the twelve sales reps, some of them new to the company, and bringing order to their redefined territories," JC told me.

"You come highly recommended, and I'm confident you're the person I need." We agreed I would start the next week, and to begin with, I would be the only clerical person in the department. I couldn't recommend additional employees until I determined what their jobs should be and how to train them.

On Monday, JC took me around the building and introduced me to the members of each department before I went to my desk just outside his office. He left me by myself to separate the chaff from the wheat, aware that I would work better alone to size things up. As I looked over my desk, the most prominent object was an old-fashioned spindle one might use to keep bits of paper from blowing away. It was overflowing with pink telephone message slips. To my dismay, I soon determined the messages were for twelve sales reps assigned to as many territories spread around the U.S. This appeared to be my predecessor's system of relaying information to and from our sales force. She was not present, having been reassigned to another department.

JC had told me that telephone communications were the most critical office function of our department. There were none of the e-mail, cell phones, or voice mail we take for granted today. Telephoning was handled by two WATS lines (Wide Area Telecommunications Service, zoned unlimited service lines) that served large businesses, often providing lifelines to widespread sales territories like Bombardier's.

Bombardier sales reps were required to telephone the office at each stop in their day as they called on their dealers. They provided daily itineraries and, if necessary, we could reach them by leaving a message at their next stop. They left messages with us enlisting help to meet their dealers' needs for parts or product orders. I sat staring for a moment at the most critical part of our sales reps' backup for dealer service—sitting in front of me, crammed on a spindle that resembled a lethal weapon.

I located a map of numbered territories, with a sales rep name in each, gingerly extracting the wad of messages from the spindle before I discarded it. I hoped the phone wouldn't ring before I could sort them out. I wasn't surprised to find they were marked only with first names (we had two Bobs) and no territory numbers, but sometimes a dealer's name was noted.

A young man approached my desk. "Hi, I'm Bob from Wisconsin. I live in Superior so I usually come in on Monday and Friday and call in on the other days. Welcome aboard—any messages?"

"I'm just starting to sort things out, but we'll soon have

a better system for your communications. I see we have two Bobs and the messages aren't too clear. I think three of them are yours, probably left over from late Friday afternoon."

"Oh yah, the other Bob is Faulkner in California. He's a good guy—the girls think he's a dead ringer for George Hamilton. You'll meet him in a few months at the next sales rep meeting."

"Thanks for your patience. I'm looking forward to working with all of you."

"It looks like you're already taking hold—you'll do fine. See you Friday."

I finished my sorting the best I could and went to the switchboard where Kathy was ready to take messages for me at coffee and lunch breaks. "Can you spell me while I run to the supply room?"

"Sure, anytime you need to leave your desk, just let me know."

Relieved, I said, "Thanks. I hope it won't be necessary too much longer, but it will be a while before we can hire another person or two."

Everyone seemed to be welcoming and willing to help. I felt at home already. In the supply room I found a large sturdy accordion folder, a box of manilla folders, and labels. I stopped by the switchboard to check with Kathy for messages before I returned to my desk. It didn't take long to label twelve folders with names and territory numbers and place them in the accordion folder. I filed the messages accordingly, making a mental note to train our new people to write complete messages with times, territory numbers, dealer names, and phone numbers. I placed the folder under my desk, out of the way, but quickly accessible. We would need to inventory and restock the supply room regularly—I had a feeling I'd be using it frequently. It was a start.

In the days that followed, I became acquainted with the sales force via telephone. Some reps had territories where dealerships were separated by long, lonely stretches of highway.

I pictured Wes Bailey, who worked in Nebraska and the Dakotas, described to me by Bobby, as a tall slim westerner with a ten-gallon hat shading a boyish face. His dealers were so far apart that sometimes he might be able to make only one call a day to send or receive messages. In one early conversation with Wes when I said, " Well, we'll talk to you later in the afternoon." Wes replied laughingly in his soft drawl, "Donna, do you know how many miles it is to my next dealer? You'll be fast asleep by the time I get there."

Time zones were another complication in our communication system. Early in my new job, I called Bob Faulkner in California to relay an urgent message. It was the first item on my "things to do Monday morning" list, before he got on the road. Oh, he was home all right; a fuzzy sounding voice croaked a weak, "Hello, who is this?"

I looked at my watch; it was 8:00 a.m. and finally remembered it was 6:00 a.m. in California. I wanted to quickly hang up, but I confessed, "It's Donna at the Duluth office; Bob I'm sorry—I was anxious to catch you before you left home, and I forgot about the time difference." He was glad to get his message, and he appreciated that communications with the field were improving and, therefore, graciously forgave my blunder.

Burgeoning Technology

Each day it became more apparent that one person couldn't handle the clerical workload of the sales department. JC had decided that he wanted me to take charge of creating new job descriptions, as well as selecting and training secretarial help for the executive offices. This process would require time I couldn't spare until we clarified the dealer listings by territory. Sales reps expressed their frustration in our phone conversations about the confused lists of dealers they received. Attempts to correct them had failed, and they didn't understand why data processing people couldn't get them straightened out.

I knew little about data processing, but I had learned one undisputed fact: The output of computer reports could be only as accurate as the input (in this case, input from the sales department). I decided to arrange a visit with Al, the data processing manager.

In its infancy, data processing was a space-consuming function. In back of our accounting department, a wall of windows enclosed a large space which housed the computer. The diva of the corporation, dust-free and temperature-controlled, it was off limits to most foot traffic. Outside the window wall, several key punchers were lined up, eyes riveted on their terminals, endlessly feeding data into one of the first computers in the city. Inside, the behemoth data processor with whirring reels digested its fodder of information and spewed it out in piles of pale green accordion pleated reports (legal size in height and double the width of regular typing paper). It held the key to redistribution of the sales territories, and provided accurate reports for all other departments of the corporation. Completed reports were encased in royal blue stiff plastic binders, labelled to use for reference, and stored on banks of shelving. I approached the door of the "sanctum" and knocked tentatively. Al looked up through glasses with wide rims that matched his dark hair. He rose and opened the door with a friendly smile and quiet greeting; "Hello, I remember we met on your first day. Can I help with anything?"

"You sure can, Al. I'm sorry I couldn't meet with you sooner, but I'm sure with an explanation of what you need from us, I can give you accurate information in short order to clarify our sales territories." After his clear and concise direction, I began immediately to erase this source of frustration which affected every aspect of our work. Each hour spent on this tedious project resulted in more accurate reporting, freeing up more time to apply to the project, and within a week, we needed very few corrections.

Some of my fellow employees were amused by my telephone manner (too formal for this business dedicated to leisure time products). One Monday morning when Bobby came in from Superior, he heard me as I answered JC's phone, "I'm sorry, he's conducting a meeting now. May I have him call you when he's finished?"

"Wow! Pretty fancy language, Donna," he laughed. This was Bobby's offhand way of offering me sound advice. I decided I'd better remember I wasn't in the bank anymore. I made a mental note to ease up on the stiff formality, inject a lighter note in phone contacts, and still maintain a professional edge.

Bobby seized the opportunity to pursue the subject of language by forewarning me about a dealer in his territory. "By the way, have you talked to my dealer Ed—the one who habitually swears when I call on him or he calls the office?"

"You mean just for the sake of swearing? Why do people put up with it?"

Bobby shrugged, "I guess we just accept it as part of Ed's personality."

"Thanks for the heads up. I'm willing to ignore it to a point, but beyond that I expect to have a civil conversation with him."

The first time I spoke with Ed on the phone, I was appalled. He didn't have a significant problem or complaint, but he swore a blue streak anyway. I let him run down and then stopped him by saying, "I'll be glad to help you, but if you want to continue this conversation, please cut down on the profanity."

This irritated him and triggered another venomous tirade, "Dammit, none of your godamned people have ever told me I couldn't swear any goddamned time I please!"

"I'm here to help you, but I'm not required to accept verbal abuse—if you continue to curse, I'll hang up." He was so startled he fell silent—I waited until he recovered and stated his business, then left his message for Bobby as requested, and the call ended on a cordial note.

On Friday morning when Bobby came into the office, he headed straight for my desk. "What did you say to Ed? He wants to know who the hell this Donna is that he can't swear at her."

Sure that Bobby didn't really expect an explanation, I replied with another question, "Gee Bobby, how did you answer that?"

"I told him he'd like you when he has a chance to get acquainted with you at the dealer meeting. Meanwhile, I suggested he watch his language."

From then on, conversations with Ed were pleasant. I think he liked finding that he could converse without resorting to profanity, and he was rewarded by warm greetings and courteous help when he called the office. When Bobby introduced him to me at my first dealer meeting, our amused coworkers, who had heard the story from Bobby, gave us sidelong looks expecting an explosion. Ed showed us a smiling, charming gentleman who, enjoying that role, became my friend and champion. He never missed an opportunity to comment on how helpful and pleasant I was when he called for information or assistance.

The language issue resurfaced in the home office. JC had asked me to sit in on his brain-storming sessions with the product managers to take notes on the ideas they kicked around. I chose a simple shorthand identification for each manager to quickly locate their comments in my notes and read them back for immediate review. Tape recording was the previous method used for this purpose. It was fast, but cumbersome. Locating the desired place on the tape to replay was intrusive on the flow of ideas. When more than one person spoke at once on tape, their voices became garbled. I could separate their comments and record them in shorthand to read back much more quickly and clearly than taping allowed.

This reminded me of the versatility of shorthand which was quickly fading from use, but maybe not entirely headed for extinction. It alerted me to keep my mind open to ways I could revive this dying art and make it work effectively for me (and possibly others) in new applications. I discerned that expertise in shorthand could enhance an executive assistant's value to a business organization.

The brain storming sessions were going so well that JC decided I should attend all meetings, including the Monday morning staff meetings. During the first staff meeting I attended, profanity reared its ugly head. One manager felt threatened by my presence, although his language around the office had always been acceptable. I had been working with him successfully, but during the meeting he began lacing his comments with profanity. I decided this must be the way he spoke among *the boys*, yet he hadn't used profanity during the brain storming sessions. When JC interrupted to remind him that we had a new member in our group and admonished him to watch his language, I realized that it was the invasion of the *Staff Meeting Sanctity*, traditionally off-limits to women, that represented a threat.

I knew that JC was intolerant of cursing in the office. Occasionally, when an out-of-patience manager burst out with, "Jee-zus Kee-rist!," he stopped them dead in their tracks by making eye contact and saying evenly, tempered with a smile, "You don't have to be so formal—just call me JC."

I appreciated his light, but effective method of dealing with cursing in front of the office employees, yet I resented his citing me as a reason for insisting on civil language at the meeting. When it ended, I followed JC into his office and closed the door firmly, stopping just short of slamming it. I could hardly wait to launch into my rant, "I've heard bad language before—I can handle it. I don't expect special treatment, and you don't have to look after me—you just reminded the guys that now they have to put up with a woman in their sacred staff meeting!"

JC quelled my outburst by saying, "Hold on, Schilling! You don't get it. He has never sworn during staff meetings, and if he had, I'd have called him on it. He was doing it just for your benefit, trying to intimidate you. He'll have to get over being scared of you and accept your being there."

I quietly removed my foot from my mouth so I could apologize and thank him meekly as I backed out of his office, closing the door quietly. JC was right; they learned to accept me, even sometimes forgetting themselves and asking for my opinion.

I realized in retrospect that this was the day I made my entree into the world of management by directing my soon-to-be-obsolete shorthand skill into new channels—and I had JC to thank for the opportunity.

It was time to contact the employment service and begin interviewing for our first additional secretary who would be assigned to Jim, the new product manager for Can Am Motorcycles. Debbie proved to be a perfect choice, and was available immediately. With her direct brown eyed gaze, well-groomed long brown hair, and open manner, she was a rare combination of charm and readiness to take care of business. JC was pleased, Jim was pleased, and I was ecstatic! I had her job description ready and she was on board.

The weeks were passing quickly, and although this multifaceted business was far removed from the marble and mahogany atmosphere of banking, I was caught up in the seemingly casual pulling together of many varied elements necessary to its success. It was every bit as serious as the banking business, yet it was comparable to the team sports I had always loved, each manager working cooperatively in a fast-paced, but cohesive network to achieve our purpose.

We were beginning to prepare for the season's big sales push, which would begin with meetings in our offices. The entire sales force in all twelve territories would attend. I had determined that we needed two additional people, one to work for Tom, the Ski-Doo manager and the other for Darryl, the Moto-Ski manager. Moto-Ski was a snowmobile acquired by Bombardier from a Japanese manufacturer. Their inventory had been shipped to our warehouse to be distributed to its dealer network by our sales reps under Darryl's supervision. I planned for each secretary to develop a speciality in their own product line, while working cooperatively to cover telephone contacts (the reps' lifeline to their home office) for one another, during breaks or absences. First, I hired Lois, an experienced woman in her fifties, to work for the Ski-Doo manager. She was capable and well-liked by the rest of the sales department. I hoped she would be up to the demands of the product representing our largest sales.

I hired Margi to work in the Moto-Ski section for Darryl. She was bright and personable and worked well with our other two choices. I was disappointed when Lois found the pace too fast for her comfort and did not stay long. We were sorry to lose her, but I quickly set about searching for her replacement. I was hoping to find a match for Debbie when I interviewed Cindy.

Cindy's story represented an unfortunate example of vulnerable women who, because they needed to work stayed in untenable jobs, intimidated by threats of *no letters of reference* when they gave their notice. She had been sent to me by an agency for the interview and I was impressed by her appearance, manner, and qualifications. As I invited her to sit down, I was aware she was not comfortable. Before she took a seat, she burst out, "I'm not sure you'll want to hire me—I won't be able to give you a recommendation from my former employer. I don't want to waste your time if that prevents you from considering me."

A pang of *deja vu* alerted me that her story was worth hearing. "First, tell me why you left your previous job."

Cindy began without hesitation. "It was my first job, and I was working for an attorney who began falling behind paying my salary. I had to keep reminding him that I hadn't been paid for the previous week. After a few months, I was wondering how to resolve the problem when he began insisting I lie to his wife regarding his whereabouts when she called. It was the last straw...I couldn't do it, and when I told him I'd be leaving, he said I'd better reconsider because I wouldn't get another job. He threatened to tell any prospective employers that I had been fired for incompetence."

She was young and shy, but had stood her ground and now sat before me hoping I might believe her. I felt the anger rise in my throat recalling my own recent experience, which paralleled her story, except we had different reasons for resigning from our jobs. I had been older, experienced and had other sources, whereas Cindy had only one source of reference and feared her boss could make good on his threat. I knew her story was true and wanted to shout my indignation, but managed to speak evenly, "Your test scores from the agency are excellent, I like what I see, and you came in and stated your situation with courage and dignity. I believe you, and I'd like you to meet Tom, our Ski-Doo Manager, the person who needs a secretary. I want the two of you to be comfortable about my choice before I offer you the job."

I introduced her to Tom, who readily approved hiring her to work for him. Later, after he thanked me for finding him the perfect secretary, I told him her story and he was as outraged as I had been. Had I not been in the same position a few months earlier, it would have been hard for me to believe any employer would use such tactics to intimidate a subordinate.

The secretarial training was my first opportunity to test the conviction that employee training was a key factor in creating satisfaction as well as efficiency in the workplace. It had been sorely lacking in my experience to date. The North Shore Bank in Lakeside had been the exception. My experience had shown that lack of training resulted in costly error and careless work. Employees got the message that if their job did not require training except in an offhand manner by the departing worker, it was not likely management paid much attention to how it was done. Often, this was the case, except when mistakes occurred and a hapless new person was blamed, and worse, reminded that they had been here three months and should know their job by now. At Bombardier, I created job descriptions to avoid misunderstandings of responsibilities, backed up by a manual outlining procedures to ensure work consistency. It served as a dependable source of reference readily available to all employees, which was important for the secretaries who were required to work without supervision when I was traveling. Moreover, working independently was vital to their personal confidence and pride in accomplishment.

I regularly consulted them before updating or adding procedures to the manual. Because they were performing the jobs, they offered the best source of suggestions. We were, after all, learning together. The sales force was appreciative of the pleasant manner and efficiency of their "lifeline."

The only problem with our training program was that our trio of secretaries, because they worked quickly and accurately, were prevailed upon by managers in other departments to help with *their* work. They had their own clerical people and should have trained them better, enlisted my help in training, or complained to the general office manager if they weren't satisfied. I understood, but had to find a tactful way to let the managers know we didn't have time to take on extra work except in an emergency. I asked the secretaries to refer requests for help to me. Women were not accustomed to saying "no" to any manager on a job, so this put the responsibility on me. The managers knew they hadn't been fair and didn't ask me for additional help, knowing what my answer would be. Then one of them went to JC asking to *use* his clerical people (one of my least favorite expressions). JC simply told them I was in charge of managing their time, so I was the one to ask. This reminded me of the kid trick of trying to wheedle Dad into overriding Mom's "no" to unreasonable requests. I learned that a few people in other departments referred to me as "Mother Superior" (not openly, of course) which was probably justified, as I did protect our secretaries from being taken advantage of. If another department truly needed help, I rearranged our workload to accommodate them. In those circumstances, when I asked any of our secretaries to help out, they were always willing to cooperate.

I was gratified that when JC gave me additional responsibilities, he also gave me the authority to carry them out without countermanding my decisions. I have worked with few management people who handled their jobs as well as this multitalented man, and he did it with grace and a great sense of humor.

One of my varied duties was one that neither JC nor I anticipated. His foremost calling was art; he had been Bombardier's clothing designer in its early days, and still added new outfits to the clothing line each season. He sketched designs of suits and accessories, which came to life at local manufacturers' factories in colors coordinated with the new models of snowmobiles and motorcycles. The sales representative for the manufacturers picked up the sketches, and within a week returned with a rack of clothing and matching accessories.

The first time a rack of new designs rolled in, JC looked them over, and said, "Schilling, they look about your size. Why don't you try one on so we can see it on a live model."

When they all proved to be my size, I caught JC off guard by asking, "Does this mean I get to add "mannequin" to my resume?"

A quick look from the corner of his eye, assured him that I was kidding, before he assembled the managers for the impromptu style show. JC's office was the dressing room and my runway was the commons area outside the executive offices where, along with managers, a number of curious onlookers from other departments got a preview of the new clothing by peeking around corners. I was grateful for JC's professional demeanor, which deterred any whistles or catcall from the sidelines.

Lighting was provided by sun streaming through the front windows turning the fabrics to liquid jet, burnt orange and intensified Ski-Doo yellow. Outfits were viewed from every angle and we considered each detail objectively, sometimes leaving favorite designs behind because they were less complementary to the sleds or impractical in color.

One of my first choices, a white suit with orange and yellow strategic striping had to be eliminated from production because of the light color. It was an inspired design and the manufacturers' rep, who was part of the viewing process, declared he was going to have the outfit custom made for me, claiming that I helped him sell his products. He measured me to insure a perfect fitting suit, and a few days later when I returned from lunch the gleaming white treasure was hanging on the door of JC's office, enhanced by sunlight reflected from the sparkling banks of snow outside. I wore it as a ski outfit for years on the Rocky Mountain slopes.

The selected samples were to accompany us (under my care) to May dealer meetings, for showing by professional models, along with slides and films as part of our presentation. Orders from dealers would be a determining factor in the number produced. Ordinarily I might have been self-conscious parading around to show off clothing, but it was part of our work and a practical solution to aid in a business decision—so we got on with it, along with some laughing and posturing. It was another completed item on the dealer meeting checklist.

Meeting the Sales Reps

During the heavy snow months, December through February, the Duluth office staff was simultaneously managing the 1974 season's business and preparing materials for a sales rep training week scheduled for late winter. Training was the first step in planning for the upcoming season almost a year away. The training week preceded a series of May dealer meetings in selected cities at which dealers viewed the new products and placed initial orders for the coming season. This year, they would also meet the new people of the reconstructed *Bombardier Corporation*, a subsidiary of *Bombardier Ltd.*, as well as greeting some familiar faces from the old Halvorson days.

Marilyn and Jack held key positions in the traffic department, and were familiar to many dealers from the Halvorson years. Marilyn's feminine stylish appearance, fair skin and dark hair with sparkling eyes and a trim figure belied her occupation. She loaded the products on paper from sales reps' orders, sketching out loads on diagrams of trailer interiors. These in turn were sent to Jack, our ruggedly handsome expert in traffic management. It was fascinating to watch Jack give clipped, clear directions to his loading crew around the large ever-present cigar clenched in his teeth. Since Marilyn coordinated the delivery date with each dealer, she had frequent phone contact with them. Her work was impeccable, making her a great favorite among them. She and I were scheduled to be traveling companions to the meetings, and together greet our dealers as they arrived.

New product information came from Montreal, which provided the specs and photos of the new lines and information for support areas of parts, service, pricing, and performance. Each department participated by lending their expertise in their own field to contribute to the training effort. My responsibility was to collect materials and assemble a sales training manual that JC would use in conducting work with his field reps. JC and the product managers prepared various parts of this manual and I became accustomed to one of them standing behind me dictating as I typed pages which I barely had time to proofread before they whisked off the original copies to be printed.

Just as the name *Ski-Doo* was used to designate any snowmobile, *Xerox* became the name universally used to designate copiers. Copiers had come a long way in a few years, and we had the latest *Xerox* model. It was operated by Tiny (not surprisingly an unusually big man) in charge of printing, who patiently duplicated much of our paperwork. Our sophisticated copier produced such fine quality work that I coaxed it to "cut and paste" seamless combinations of words and illustrations for use in our manuals. Larger printing jobs were sent out to a local professional printer.

By the end of February, we were prepared to launch our week of training sessions. The marketing department had arranged transportation and hotel accommodations for the sales group and set up a kickoff dinner meeting and get-acquainted time at what is now the Holiday Center. Management people from all departments of the Duluth staff were invited to meet the sales reps in person for the first time, an opportunity to solidify the communication network maintained by telephone.

The stage was set and they converged on Duluth from all parts of the country, Bobby Brennan and Bill Agenter from Duluth and Superior were familiar, but the other ten had been, until now, voices on the WATS line. Gary Becker, Brian Seaman, and Jerry Halstead from Michigan (a big snow state); Wes Bailey from Nebraska and the Dakotas, with their sparse population; Big Sol Salveson from Utah; John Foschi from southern Minnesota; and Dave Paron from Minneapolis.

Bill Agenter, Duluth Sales Rep, with Donna, ca. 1980.

Bill McConville, our *Can Am* Motorcycle rep arrived from sunny Atlanta, Jack Erickson from Colorado, and of course from California, Bob Faulkner whose dreams I had disturbed by calling at 6:00 a.m.

A program followed the dinner where JC introduced the group and outlined the series of meetings where, in the coming week, our new Bombardier sales staff would become saturated with information about the new product lines. Training was for tomorrow—this evening was for socializing and getting to know each other in a less hectic setting than we usually shared. So now began an amusing comparison between our phone impressions and how people looked in person. Gary began by saying, "I talked to Bobby one day when I called Duluth, and I asked him what JC's new secretary was like. He told me she was middled-aged, efficient, and a former banker. When I asked,

'But how does she look?' he said, 'JC hires people for capability, not looks.' Bobby, you were pulling my leg!"

"Hey, wait a minute; did I lie?" Bobby spoke up, and I had to verify the truth of his description, although I also said, "Well Bobby, you could have at least made me sound a little more interesting."

The word had gotten round (probably justified) that I was dull, but capable. Bobby took the good-natured ribbing and readily acknowledged, with an eye-twinkling smile, that maybe he had sold me short in his description.

For those of us who spoke to them every day, we were surprised to find the sales force did not all fit their voices. Some had been described to me by others; boyish-looking Wes with his tall hat and slow drawl was just as I pictured him. Bob, was a ringer for George, but his healthy California tan wasn't close to the deep mahogany shade of Hamilton's. Now he had a chance to razz me in person about the wakeup call a few months earlier. I'd heard about "Big Sol," but wasn't prepared for this soft-spoken huge teddy bear of a man. Looking at Gary, short and stocky, I wouldn't have suspected he was the par golfer that he was. Jack Erickson, who brought me a gift of an unusual piece of driftwood from the mountains of Colorado, was a man of few words. But Bobby, who had worked a few days with Jack in Colorado, reported fearing for his life as The Quiet Man careened around the switchbacks in the Colorado Rockies.

They were all curious about the secretaries they spoke to daily. "Are they really as great in person as they sound on the phone?" I was happy to reassure them, "Yes they are lovely, efficient, and eager to meet you all in person tomorrow."

The sales reps were also happy to meet the rest of the backup team at the home office during the week of training. Then they were back to their territories, and plans continued at an accelerated pace for the May dealer meetings. Each of our assignments were much the same as they had been for our week of sales training, except that the volume increased dramatically. Packets for each dealer were prepared containing much of the same information we had given our sales reps. Most of it was prepared by me, working with the sales managers; what I didn't type myself, I collected from the various other departments, assembling it all in special binders designed at the factory and shipped earlier in the year.

Our marketing people, Bob and Carol planned the presentation with film and slides to be coordinated with live models showing the clothing, and the display of new sleds and motorcycles. The meetings were held in large hotels with accommodations for industrial showings, with arrangements also handled by Bob and Carol. They reserved blocks of rooms for dealers and the Bombardier people designated to be present, along with airline reservations to transport our staff to the meeting site.

Two northwestern cities were selected where we repeated the presentation on three consecutive days in each city to accommodate the entire dealer network. Warren, our president insisted we split up the staff to fly in small groups in case of a plane crash, which added to the complexity of logistics for Bob and Carol. Since I was sure that lost luggage was more likely than a crash, I took the precaution of packing an uncrushable dinner dress in my carryon case in the event my luggage didn't arrive with us.

Jerry Calengor, Bombardier Corporation Sales Manager, pictured here (right) with a Halvorson Ski-Doo Distributors coworker, ca. 1967.

The day before the first May dealer meeting, our loading dock was alive with activity—organized chaos, under the capable direction of Jack Leicht, the warehouse manager. Staff members, who were responsible for their materials, stood waiting to see them loaded aboard a Halvor Lines rig. The air of anticipation was heightened by the tractor's pulsing motor, impatient to get on the road with its loaded trailer and be at the meeting site when we arrived. I had dealer packets and the rack of clothing samples at hand, waiting with the others for Jack to bark orders around the stub of cigar held in his teeth directing fork lift operators wheeling Ski-Doo crates from warehouse to trailer, then finally to load the smaller gear, freeing us from guard duty. Anything that couldn't be carried on planes went aboard. By the time it arrived at the appointed city, all of us from sales, service, warranty, marketing, and the floor planning group, would arrive to meet the truck and each retrieve their materials and have them placed in the designated area at the meeting facility. We also had our personal luggage, which eventually found its way to our rooms.

Phil Mickelson conducting a Bombardier service class, ca. 1967.

Marilyn and I working together, wasted no time in arranging dealer packets alphabetically on the entry table. When the first dealers arrived at 3:00 p.m., we were ready to greet them with our best smiles as we pinned on their name tags.

Meetings for a number of Minnesota and Wisconsin dealers were held in Minneapolis. On one of those occasions, we met at a large hotel which offered a dinner theater in a dining area close to our meeting room. When we brought in our rack of clothing, we discovered we would share a dressing room with the actors appearing in the current dinner theatre production. We saw no problem with that since our show would be finished long before theirs began. We placed the clothing in our assigned space and our presentation went off without a hitch. I had assembled the clothing on the rack in the order it would appear, and the models had made their clothing changes on cue, timed perfectly to work with the film and slides, and the dealers approved the new line. The dinner was excellent, and the sales group was tired, but happy as we moved into the lounge to relax over a nightcap. We were congratulating one another on how well our first of the three Minneapolis meetings had gone, when someone said, "JC, isn't that one of our sweaters?"

In unison, we looked over toward the bar where the thespians from the dinner theatre were clustered congratulating themselves on *their* performances. We stared in disbelief at a handsome blond actor sporting a newly designed sample *Ski-Doo* sweater. We all stood up and moved nearer. JC approached the actor and told him the sweater was becoming, but we needed it for our presentation the next day. The young man indignantly declared it belonged to him and refused to take it off. When JC informed him that the sweater was his design and none had yet been sold, the actor gave up arguing ownership, but brazenly replied, "Then I'm sure you have plenty of them— you won't miss just this one."

It was the one sweater of that design in existence, and production would be based on how well it was received by the dealers. JC was losing patience, but said evenly, "No it's a sample, and necessary to our show tomorrow." When the young man laughed and started to turn away, JC said, "If you don't want to take it off yourself, I'd be glad to help you." He remained calm, but his smile was cold, the chill reflecting in his eyes.

At that point Tom, the *Ski-Doo* manager, anticipating fisticuffs to develop between The Thespians and The Boys from Bombardier, moved in front of me and said, "Schilling stay behind me and don't move!" It was beginning to resemble the showdown scene of a saloon brawl from an old western movie, where the villain is caught red-handed cheating at cards.

Evidently The Thespians didn't like the odds; the arrogant young actor carefully eased the sweater over his well-coifed blond curls and handed it over to JC without another word. The next morning, we had some concern about the overnight security of our clothing collection, but found it untouched. JC replaced the retrieved sweater in the empty slot and the show went on.

An impromptu image of Donna,
sketched by Jerry Calengor during
a tedious meeting, ca. 1977.

Return to Montreal

The time was nearing when the young Duluth Corporation would be phased out. There had been talk about people from Montreal coming to Duluth to take over the management of the U.S. distributorship. Instead, within a few years after its opening, Bombardier Corporation was moved to Montreal to become part of Bombardier Ltd. Some of our people stayed in Duluth for a short time; others moved to larger cities. JC accepted a position in Minneapolis until retirement, when he returned to his first love of art, which keeps him, as he says, "Too busy to call it retirement." I have enjoyed seeing one of his recent paintings in the lobby of the North Shore Bank in Lakeside where I began working in 1967 and am now back as a customer.

The service manager, Phil Mickelson, who had also worked for the Halvorson Company before Bombardier Corporation was formed, continued in the Duluth facility until the building lease ran out during the transition to Montreal. Phil's last service to Bombardier was rendered in 2009, long after he closed the doors on Bombardier Corporation. The first Ski-Doo shipped to Halvorson in 1960 remained in his care. I am grateful to Phil for allowing me to reprint the following history of *that little yellow Ski-Doo* on wooden skis told in his own words.

**** February 1, 2009 News Release****

VALUABLE SKI-DOO ARRIVES IN ST. GERMAIN
...Phil Mickelson, now retired, but formerly with the Halvorson organization of Duluth, Minnesota has been the caretaker of the early *Ski-Doo* and wrote the following history of the sled...**1960 Ski-Doo model K60, serial number 60290, engine serial number 439776. Kohler 4 stroke-cycle, 7hp...**

Vintage Ski-Doo History

by Phil Mickelson

This is a very special 1960 Ski-Doo! Roy Halvorson of Duluth, Minnesota, created a business known as Halvorson Tree Co. in 1929. He harvested black spruce trees from peat bogs and swamps, today we call them wetlands, in northern Minnesota and Canada, removed their beautiful tops and treated them to reduce transpiration, hold their needles, and enhance their color; added a nutrient filled base and shipped them all over the world as living Christmas trees.

Harvesting the trees meant operating in the peat bogs of northern Minnesota and hauling the trees out of the bogs was a difficult operation. Roy had employed everything from horses to wide tracked Caterpillar tractors to move his product. He had heard of a company in Valcourt, Quebec that was building a soft-terrain machine that just might do the job for him. Roy tracked down a Bombardier dealer in Cochran, Ontario, in 1955 and purchased one of the Bombardier, Ltd.'s Muskeg tractors and had it shipped to him. The tractor proved to be a smashing success, and Roy quickly realized how valuable it was to his company and the salability of this versatile machine.

In 1956, Roy Halvorson flew his Aero Commander airplane to Montreal, Quebec, Canada, drove to Valcourt and met with Armand Bombardier. Upon realizing that Armand spoke no English and Roy spoke no French, Armand referred Roy to Armand's brother, Alphonse-Raymond who could converse comfortably in English. Roy was able to set up a distributorship for Bombardier's products in Duluth, Minnesota, and founded Halvorson Forest Equipment Co. to be headed by his son, Tom, who had recently graduated from college.

The tracked vehicles from Bombardier performed admirably and Halvorson Forest Equipment grew rapidly. In the late summer or early fall of 1959, a rail shipment of tractors from Bombardier included a strange little yellow machine named Ski-Doo. Neither Roy nor Tom said they had ordered the machine and noted that Armand had probably shipped it to them on speculation that it might arouse their sales instincts. Roy argued with Charles Leblanc, Bombardier's chief legal consultant over whether or not they ever really ordered that first Ski-Doo or if it was just shipped as a sample.

The Halvorsons really didn't know who or what the market was for the little machine and simply unloaded it and stored it in their tractor repair shop in Duluth. In March of 1960, Harland Rousse, manager of the tractor shop, asked to have the little machine removed from the shop so he could use the space it occupied.

Tom Halvorson had it moved to his garage in Duluth. His home was adjacent to the Northland Country Club in Duluth, a private golf club with lots of open territory and a lot of elevation change. Tom cleaned the dust and dirt off the machine, urged by John Hoff Jr, fired it up and took it out on the golf course on the sparse snow that was remaining. He had an absolute ball with the machine!

Tom was smiling from ear to ear that next Monday, and announced that the Ski-Doo was really a fun machine! Roy and other employees of the company and friends rode the strange little Ski-Doo as soon as they could. Everyone was thrilled with what this little machine could do, and it was then that Tom and Roy realized that this was not an industrial or work machine, like those they had been marketing, but a big boy toy that was really fun to ride when there wasn't much else to do to have fun in the winter.

This particular machine, serial number 60290, is that first Ski-Doo shipped to the midwest of the United States, and is the machine that turned Tom and Roy Halvorson's attention from industrial applications to recreational applications.

This is also the first Ski-Doo sold by Halvorson Forest Equipment. It was originally sold to John Bero of Duluth, Minnesota, who "just wanted it to play around with." Roy Halvorson, several years later, bought that first Ski-Doo back, knowing it had a special place in the history of snowmobiling. This sled was on display at Halvorson Incorporated's office until they were purchased by "Bombardier, Inc." in 1973. The sled was then displayed in the entry of Bomardier Corp's office in Duluth until they moved to Wausau, Wisconsin, in 1991.

When Bombardier's Duluth distribution center was shut down, I was left in charge of the building until the lease expired. Our service department and several service operations that were still functioning in Duluth were then moved to Wausau, Wisconsin.

I knew the entire history of this 1960 Ski-Doo that I had walked past every day for twenty-four years, and wasn't about to let it leave Duluth. I kept this Ski-Doo in Duluth and later contacted Tom Halvorson to see if he wanted to have it back. He said that he would rather see it in a significant museum.

In 1976, I had worked with Randy Mason, Curator of Transportation at the Henry Ford Museum and Greenfield Village, Dearborn, Michigan. The museum has a 1961 Ski-Doo in their display. The Ford Museum is one of the largest museums in the world, and I had thought it might be a great home for this first production run Ski-Doo. The problem was, Detroit was not in the original Halvorson distribution territory. Lower Michigan was provided Ski-Doo distribution by Brooks Equipment, based in Richmond, Michigan.

As I looked for a permanent home for this historic Ski-Doo, I looked to St. Germain, Wisconsin, at the Snowmobile Hall of Fame. They already had an incredible collection of very special sleds, and this original Ski-Doo, with its incredible background, will be on display at the Snowmobile Hall of Fame for all of snowmobile history.

January 23, 2009

PART SIX

LIFE AT ENTERPRISES

A Voice From the Past

A few days after Thanksgiving in 2011, I was in the kitchen preparing dinner when a familiar voice came from the TV in my living room. Startled, I realized the speaker from my past was Jeno Paulucci, responding to a young woman interviewer's question on how he acquired his wealth and became so successful in business. He was saying, "I've had plenty of failures. I don't want anyone to get the idea I didn't make mistakes." He went on to cite an example of a failure to pick up on a wonderful deal, "On a trip with my wife Lois, I was offered an opportunity to buy into a professional team that I turned down without a second glance. I thought they'd never amount to anything. After they turned out to be big winners, Lois never let me hear the end of it."

Chuckling at some embarrassing moments brought forth by his recollections, he told of a sales pitch early in his Chun King days when he personally called on merchants to try to place his canned Chinese vegetables on their shelves.

"There was only one other producer of canned Chinese products in the country, and I wanted a share of that market. I pitched my bean sprouts to a retailer in Wisconsin—he was wavering, so I opened a can to show him. There on top of the sprouts was a big grasshopper. I grabbed the grasshopper along with some bean sprouts, looking him in the eye as I popped them in my mouth, chewed them up, and swallowed them, telling him they were good enough to eat right from the can! You have to work hard and be able to think on your feet to make a business go!"

Jeno F. Paulucci, 1967.
Photo: Minnesota Historical Society

The interview broadcast with Jeno was not unusual—
he was legendary in the state of Minnesota as one of its most
prominent and wealthiest entrepreneurs. So—what took me
aback at the sound of his voice in my living room that day? Jeno
and his wife Lois had just passed away within four days of one
another over the Thanksgiving holiday, marking the end of their
wonderful private love story. Jeno's death marked the end of an
era in Duluth's business history, and a little piece of my heart
went with him as I remembered how much fun he was to work
with.

Behind the Double Doors

My snowmobile days over, in the late 1970s and early
1980s I worked at Paulucci Enterprises, a group of ten to twelve

people who handled the administrative business of Jeno's personal holdings. Our offices were housed in a building on Lake Avenue at the harbor. The red oval sign over the front door I entered each morning read simply **JENO'S**. In addition to our offices, the building contained the entire Jeno's, Inc. frozen pizza company Jeno created and owned after selling his Chun King frozen food company to R. J. Reynolds. Jeno's was as close as any building could get to the Aerial Bridge. The water from St. Louis Bay lapped against the retaining wall enclosing the small grass plot beyond the brick building. On Lake Avenue, early risers might see a garage door slide open soundlessly to swallow up a long, black luxury car with tinted windows. As the door slid shut, Jeno's day began, usually before anyone else had arrived.

The front entry took the visitor up a short flight of stairs to a large reception area. Just to the right of the stairs were wide double doors opening on the suite of offices called *Pauluci Enterprises*. Many people avoided the double doors if they could, intimidated by the powerhouse personality behind them. The offices were not sumptuous, but pleasant and roomy, unlike the cubby holes where people work in many places today.

Usually, few Jeno's, Inc. employees came through the double doors except department heads, who attended weekly staff meetings in Jeno's combination office-conference room. Most other members of Jeno's, Inc. staff who had offices on the first floor, avoided our space, referring to it as "Behind the Double Doors," many of them declaring, "I wouldn't work behind those double doors for anything." Part of their intimidation stemmed from Jeno's penchant for outbursts of colorful language when his quick temper was aroused sending expletives tumbling down the short spiral staircase from his office and through our corridor.

What those outside the double doors *didn't* know was that the shouted expletives weren't directed to the secretarial staff, but were transmitted to unseen recipients by telephone, or were recorded in shorthand notebooks to be transcribed into scathing memos and letters. Although he might be hard on his managers, we who communicated his words were exempt from his wrath. A common phrasing by businessmen of that era, "Have your girl call my girl to make an appointment," was an obscenity Jeno never uttered. He had too much respect for us to use that expression of implied ownership, and referred to us by name. He also trusted us implicitly, I believe a rarity in bosses (then and now).

My role at Paulucci Enterprises was that of secretary to Bob Heller, Jeno's personal attorney. Bob dictated his work on an electronic tape machine. He dropped the tapes on my desk, to be transcribed though an earphone attached to the receiver. It was becoming unusual to find executives who worked directly with a secretary. Like Bob, they often liked to use time on planes to catch up on correspondence via small Dictaphones. When I was interviewed by Bob, he inquired if I would be comfortable taking dictation from Jeno, who preferred dictating directly to a secretary. He often simply dictated from his private Falcon jet by radio phone to the office for as long as he was within range. He staggered the work schedules of his secretary Gail and me to extend his working day by an hour. I came in earlier than Gail and she worked later. I was confident in my command of Gregg Shorthand, and I was sure Jeno would keep me in practice. Bob explained that Jeno's work came first with everyone in our group, and if he requested my help, Bob assured me his own paperwork could wait.

The first time Jeno asked me to write a memo for him, he told me to write everything he dictated—just the way he said it. Puzzled that he felt the need to add that instruction, I assured him I would. He began dictating and it was soon apparent that he was frustrated with the intended recipient of his letter. As he warmed up to his topic, the goddamns and for chrissakes increased with the velocity of the dictation, which I obediently recorded word-for-word. When he finished, he said in his normal voice, but looking at me closely, "I hope I didn't scare you with that language."

"No Jeno, you didn't scare me, but I believe that overuse of expletives causes them to lose their effectiveness, so I make a practice of writing only one per sentence—if that's okay with you. (I offered this to share one of the benefits of my impeccable private secretary training.)

Disarmed, he looked at me for a few seconds before answering—then he broke into a smile and allowed that it made sense. That set the tone for our working relationship, which remained mutually harmonious for its duration.

Typically our dictation sessions began with Jeno buzzing my intercom and politely asking, "Donna, could you take a note for me?" The "note" was inevitably two or three pages long with the volume of his voice increasing in direct proportion to the heat of his topic. When he finished, he said, "Thank you, Donna," with a smile, as I left his office to transcribe it. Jeno knew exactly how long it took for me to complete the typing, and appeared at my desk with hand extended just as I removed the paper from my typewriter. It was a mystery how that worked, because he had started down the spiral staircase before the sound of my typewriter stopped.

We knew his displeasure wasn't directed toward us. He never raised his voice to us, so we took no offense at the tone of his "working voice." As absorbed as he was in his work, he often took the time to buzz the intercom shortly after a dictating session with a compliment.

"I really appreciate the accuracy and quality of your work. Thank you," or he might say, "I've worked with secretaries of big shot attorneys in the twin cities, and their work isn't nearly as good as yours." Jeno usually moved very fast and didn't waste a motion, yet he considered acknowledgement of quality work a valid use of his time.

Occasionally Jeno surprised me, and I failed to have a shorthand book within reach. One morning he buzzed just as I hung up my coat. I had taken out a stack of work and placed the morning paper on top of it. He started dictation over the phone just as I grabbed for a pen and began writing his "note" in the margin of the newspaper. I had a large pad of tear-off sheets on my desk in lieu of a blotter, and as his momentum increased, I shoved the stack of folders off my desk onto the floor to continue writing on the desk pad, which had no lines to guide the placement of symbols. I quickly transcribed the memo from the margin of the newspaper and the desk pad before I forgot the gist of the message. When Jeno came down the steps with his hand outstretched, he was chuckling, "A little problem getting started this morning, Donna?" He was looking at the pile on the floor and the haphazard substitute shorthand pad. I handed him his memo, "Yes Jeno, I seem to have run out of shorthand pads."

"Nothing stops you, does it?"

"Not much, Jeno."

If any of the messengers who handled the mail and distributed information throughout our building had qualms about working with Jeno, they were quickly dispelled. They soon found the offices beyond the double doors well within their comfort zone and moved in and out of them many times daily with an equanimity never realized by some of the managers of the company. Jeno appeared in the mailroom before any of the messengers began their day, and they became accustomed to finding him there sorting through the huge volume of mail, selecting pieces that required his urgent attention. They quickly learned to work companionably and developed an easy relationship with him based on mutual respect of working people for one another. When he left the mailroom he took his treasure trove to his office to prepare for a dictation session on my arrival.

There was one occasion when a new messenger worked up the courage to approach my desk and ask, "Donna, who is the man who comes in the mailroom every morning. He usually wears a red golf shirt, blue jeans, and cowboy boots."

"That's Jeno."

"I kinda' thought so—but I didn't dare ask him."

"He wouldn't have minded. By the way, call him Jeno—never Mr. Paulucci."

"Really. Gee, Thanks!"

He expected everyone to call him "Jeno," and if anyone made the mistake of calling him Mr. Paulucci, he corrected them with a friendly growl, "My name is JENO!"

What About Bob?

At this point the reader may ask, "Well, what about *Bob*? Wasn't he the busy attorney you were hired to work for?" Bob's emphasis was on Jeno's work coming first, and it was imperative that I felt comfortable working with Jeno, within our close-knit group. It, therefore, seemed appropriate to start with an introduction to Jeno, the hands-on dynamo who kept the wheels turning.

Bob became my top candidate for the ideal boss. He had detailed his expectations during our first conversation, and his demands never exceeded my job description. In contrast to Jeno, he was self-contained and soft-spoken with a pleasant, but professional manner. He excelled in his business, which he conducted adroitly without excessive legalese cluttering his language—a refreshing quality. In the years I worked with Bob he never expected me to take responsibility for *his* work.

Paulucci Enterprises Attorney Bob Heller and his wife Lois, ca. 1979.

This was reinforced in a conversation we had when he hired an intern to work in our office for the summer. Bob and I had been working on our annual updating of files, which required reorganizing of the file cabinets in my office (tedious work). He planned to have the student assist with this task under my direction. I had noticed that the student, full of his new-found knowledge, regarded me as a robot that typed.

"Bob, I don't think he will be pleased to have me telling him..."

Bob's sunny smile told me he knew exactly what I was about to say, stopping me in mid-sentence. He began speaking in his usual low-key manner. "That's too bad—he needs to learn some lessons that you can provide, the same as I did when I was clerking." He went on to cite some lessons to be learned as a clerk, "Some legal work seems mundane and easy to pass on to secretaries—work that is the responsibility of the attorney who should attend to it personally. We have updated the files together, and now he can learn how that should be done at year's end, as he helps reassemble them. It will stand him in good stead in years to come."

Bob talked about spending his summers during law school clerking in an attorney's office where the firm's secretary and office manager helped him immensely. She had helped shape his convictions of how a good attorney handles his work, something that wasn't detailed in law school. Although she was capable of drafting legal documents and numerous procedures that were the attorney's work, they had not delegated any of their legal responsibilities to her. In my years of experience, I had seen a number of examples of lawyers blaming their "girls" for errors in client's work. I realized how fortunate both the student and I were to spend this time working with Bob.

As Jeno's attorney, Bob traveled frequently, often with Jeno, who maintained an office in Florida where he held extensive real estate. Jeno kept in touch with our office by telephone when he was away, dictating work long distance, often from the air as he traveled on his Falcon jet, the first Duluthian to use a private jet for business travel. He loved his work which he could extend during flight time. On the Falcon, Bob dictated his work on tapes, which on his return were turned over to me for transcription.

My job was comparable with my past experience, including its confidential nature. My early training emphasizing the wisdom of considering all business transactions confidential, proved its value over the years. Neither Bob, nor Jeno ever cautioned me about, or asked me if I understood, the confidentiality of my work, an indication of their inherent trust in the office staff they selected.

I routinely scheduled my vacation in the winter months to take advantage of ski season in Colorado. Our dear friends, Joan and Bill Smith spent a month each year at their winter home on Snowmass, ten miles out of Aspen, and Hartley and I spent a week each year skiing with them. One year when snowstorms abounded in the West, Bob seemed surprised when I returned on schedule saying, "Considering the great snow, I am surprised you didn't find yourself snowbound and extend your vacation. It's a long trip to the mountains, and we could have managed a few more days if you had wanted to stay longer."

This was a new experience—"I wouldn't think of doing that."

"Remember, you work hard here, and it would be fine to call in and ask for a few more days to enjoy an exceptional snow year." What a remarkable boss. He knew I considered the Rockies my pinnacle of existence. In those years, there was still room for one to be alone at the top of High Alpine in pristine silence for a moment in time—at the top of the world. I knew it was a privilege relatively few people enjoyed.

Our location at Canal Park became another perk of my job, making "time out" enviable. On fine days, I ate bag lunches on a selected bench at the ship canal watching boat traffic from ports of call around the world. Afterward, a walk down the pier was often air-conditioned by a lake breeze, good preparation for an afternoon's work. Wednesday afternoons offered a pleasant interlude between the workday and heading home. Traditionally, that was (and still remains) the day our local boat club sails its crafts through the canal to the delight of residents who stop what they're doing to watch the graceful sails move onto Lake Superior to begin their weekly sailboat races.

On winter days I usually opted for our cafeteria, which served three meals a day to accommodate the people at *Jeno's, Inc.* who worked varied shifts. The excellent meals were subsidized by Jeno, keeping worker's costs to a minimum. The cafeteria was open to everyone who worked in the building. When Jeno's son Mick, renovated the building across the street to house the first *Grandma's Saloon and Deli*, we had another lunch option.

Jeno had created a retreat on the shores of Lake Kabetogama called *The Wilderness Lodge*, where he entertained business associates, and conducted business meetings of employees. All the comforts of home were offered in a rustic setting, where guests enjoyed fishing, boating, and relaxing in peaceful surroundings with a welcoming staff, including a great chef. The Enterprises group occasionally were invited for a weekend of relaxation at the lodge. I was sure Jeno was happiest when he was working, but was excellent at providing fun and relaxation for his guests.

Donna and Hartley, with a group from Paulucci Enterprises, arrive at Jeno's Wilderness Lodge for a weekend of relaxation, ca. 1980.

PART SEVEN

GRANDMA'S INC.

Lateral Move

When I left my job I didn't really leave *Paulucci Enter-prises*. *Grandma's Saloon and Deli* (which is hereafter referred to as simply, *Grandma's*) was one of the Enterprises that was expanding quickly. When Andy, now *Grandma's* president, asked if I could give them a little time to help with organization during this expansion, Bob said it was up to me. He was willing to give up some of my time to help with this new business, but he respected my feelings about taking on something that hadn't been included in my job description.

Grandma's Marathon had exploded into a major event in the city, and a building was acquired to house a new *Grandma's* in Minneapolis, which led to incorporation and the need for a full-time organizer on *Grandma's* corporate staff. Andy asked if I would be willing to make my few days at *Grandma's* a permanent job. It was a challenge I couldn't resist, and Bob agreed when I assured him I would find a good replacement for myself, someone who could work with Jeno as well. I located one of the best secretaries I had trained in the past, and asked if she might be interested in a challenging job replacing me. Cindy was settled in at my desk before I took on my new responsibilities as *Grandma's, Inc.* office administrator. A gruff Jeno confronted me with, "So, you're leaving us?"

"Not really," I replied. "I thought we were all working for the same purpose, and *Grandma's is* one of the *Enterprises* group."

"I know," he growled—"But we'll miss you around our offices."

I would soon return to Jeno's building when a suite for *Grandma's* management staff was created on the other side of the wall from the *Paulucci Enterprises* suite.

Rosa Reminisces

Five years ago or thereabouts two enterprising sports
Were collecting antiques by the score according to reports.
What are Mick and Andy up to now? The local wags would ask,
Their purpose soon would be revealed as they set about their
       task.

They'd open a new restaurant, including in the scheme,
The use of their collection to reflect an old-time theme.
Unaware its popularity would spread so wide and far,
They remodeled an old landmark known to all as
       "The Sand Bar."

From the day the doors were opened it was a certainty,
In our fair city, Grandma's would become the place to be.
'Though success was gratifying, Mick and Andy weren't content,
They found a boxcar for a stage and bought a circus tent.
Where entertainers could perform and audiences thrill,
While protected from the rain and Lake Superior's icy chill.

Yet Grandma's secret of success most people will agree,
Is her staff which really demonstrates her personality.
Casual relaxation is the message they convey,
Whatever effort is required, they make it seem like play.

But their talents do not end there, and before the tent we fold,
We thought we'd turn it over to Grandma's staff, and hold
       this little party for their friends and families to see
A demonstration of our people's versatility.

So, settle back—relax, we hope that each of you enjoys
Tonight's display of talent starring Rosa's girls and boys!

Donna Schilling
November 2, 1980

Playtime at Grandma's

Grandma's girls surround legendary Grandma Brocci and "Manager" portrayed by Sandy and Dennis Brennan, Halloween, ca. 1976.

Donna with Buddy Hacket who entertained at Mick's 30th birthday party, ca. 1980.

The Grandma's Duluth staff on Beer Garden stage during a break in Oktoberfest decorating party, ca. 1978.

Grandma's Marathon

Preparations for the third Grandma's Marathon were in full swing when I moved to *Grandma's, Inc.* Registrations had increased from one hundred and fifty runners to over three thousand and the City of Duluth, aware that the race could become a major event with significant economic impact, had encouraged promotion of the race by organizers and sponsors. My first year, I observed carefully every aspect of the *Grandma's* operation as I mentally prepared myself for the organizational demands of the coming year. *Grandma's II* in Minneapolis was on the drawing board and plans included renovation of the selected site the next spring.

We needed someone to help in the office with the amount of typing required to prepare for the next years of increasing numbers of marathon runners. I called the Minnesota Human Resources Department agent to seek prospects for a typist. My contact offered to send a young male applicant with impressive credentials, who could begin work immediately. I knew that typists had been men back at the turn of the century, but it was unusual to find male typists in modern offices. "This young man tested at ninety-two words a minute with no errors," she told me.

"Can you send him over today for an interview?"

"I can have him there within the hour," she replied.

I had never known anyone who tested that well. Jim, who did arrive within the hour was twenty years old, personable, well-dressed, attractive, and presented his qualifications before he asked about salary (that was refreshing). He seemed too good to be true in a world where employers were lucky to find one or two of his qualities in a candidate.

His work was nearly flawless, and his ambition was to become a secretary. He settled into his job and handled with aplomb the comments of employees who considered him to be out of place in an office. He maintained a pleasant attitude and sense of humor, overlooking the critical observations of some coworkers. I also hired a young woman to share the office duties, and they made an ideal team. Some of the other secretaries in the building, threatened by his obvious skill, showed open resentment toward Jim, commenting that he was taking a job from a woman. In recent years, it had been the lament of a number of men that women were encroaching on their territory. Why shouldn't men have equal opportunity to fill positions that had been traditionally held by women?

I talked to Jim privately and simply explained I had had a similar experience. "Jim, I know you are getting some flack from women who feel threatened by your presence, and you seem to handle it well. It isn't personal; I have had the same problem with men who disliked my working in what they considered 'male' territory. Try to smile, suggest the world is changing, and ignore efforts to argue the point. That worked better for me than verbal challenges. Just know that you're doing a good job for us, and that's what matters. Keep your cool, and they will learn to accept you."

Jim answered with a smile.

"Thanks. That makes me feel better. I know I'm in an unusual spot, but I think it's going okay so far."

During registrations for the fourth Grandma's Marathon, Jim would prove to be my mainstay in entering the information in Jeno's computer, as required for the Honeywell timing system. Jim stayed with it until every entry was completed without error. His work was a key accomplishment in our first year of working with Honeywell.

The dream of running a marathon along Lake Superior began in the 1970s. A running club called *The North Shore Striders* favored the route along the north shore for their regular course, imagining a marathon race from Two Harbors to Duluth. They found no one in the business community interested in sponsoring such an event until they approached Mick the owner, and Andy the manager, of the recently opened *Grandma's*. The *Striders'* vision captured the imagination of the two entrepreneurs, and in June of 1977, one hundred and fifty racers had run the first *Grandma's Marathon*.

Schilling is Marathon head

Donna Schilling, a three-year employee of Grandma's Inc., has been appointed Grandma's Marathon Race Administrator, according to company President Andy Borg, Jr.

The course consisted of a starting line close to Two Harbors, a series of aid stations along the route, and the finish line very close to *Grandma's* on First Avenue East at Canal Park. Support services for the marathon involved distribution of runners' packets, a kickoff spaghetti dinner in a large tent at *Grandma's*, locating tables and chairs to accommodate the tent diners, communications along the route, ambulance readiness, traffic control, a medical tent at Grandma's, transportation of racers from Duluth to starting line, trucks to carry runners' personal belongings from starting line to a secure spot at Canal Park where runners could retrieve them after the race.

My first note was that we must begin preparing for the fourth year the day after the running of race three and continue through the year. The Honeywell Company had devised a timing system for the Boston Marathon, and Andy had already contacted them to see if they would consider taking on the timing for Grandma's. Honeywell was cautious about adding to the few prestigious marathons they had on their schedule, but they were interested enough to invite Andy to Honeywell headquarters in Boston to meet with the team who created the timing system. Jeno's, Inc. used Honeywell computer equipment which could be easily accessed for the timing function. Exact timing was the critical element in marathon races to attract world class runners and expand the number of entrants by thousands. Honeywell agreed to take on the timing of Grandma's beginning the next year, the key to Grandma's future success as a top-rated race.

To handle the increasing numbers of participants, we mapped out segments of the course and support systems designating a manager for each segment. Dr. Jacott at Lakeside Clinic in Duluth, who was interested in sports medicine, agreed to staff the medical tent and direct this key operation. Jerry from Two Harbors, the starting line director from the beginning, continued with that assignment. Finish line preparations which Andy would continue to direct, included most of the management staff of *Grandma's I*. Scott, the race director, would work with the police department on traffic control, continue to direct the *Striders* aid station setup, and recruit top runner participation. Grandma's restaurant managers were responsible for the tent setup and, of course, the huge spaghetti dinner. As the race administrator, I handled budgeting, the Honeywell timing communications, the registration process, and followed the progress on each segment of the race.

I met regularly with a Honeywell team in Minneapolis who were expert in the timing process. We met in Duluth or Minneapolis, and sometimes halfway between in Hinckley. As we began accepting runner registrations, our ace typist, Jim, proved to be a great asset with his speed and accuracy, entering the data into Jeno's computer system for every contestant with no errors.

Meetings of all other committees related to the race were held regularly. I assembled written materials from leaders of each planning group to include in the race packets as necessary. Each runner, on their arrival in Duluth, received a packet explaining every aspect of the event. The logistics were mind-boggling, so we contemplated the race in segments rather than whole—that would be overwhelming. *Grandma's* staff considered each part of the process at Monday morning meetings. Members of the management staff reported on progress in their assigned areas. Andy might ask, "Donna, have you figured out how we can identify the triage workers in the medical tent for Dr. Jacott?"

"I've been looking for armbands in every sporting goods outlet I can think of. It will be faster to go to the mall, buy some stretchy fabric and sew them myself, color coding the workers to designate doctor, nurse, aides, and whoever else Dr. Jacott wants us to identify."

"How will you know what sizes?"

"They'll be stretchy and I'll do a variety of small, medium, and large in every color. I'll finish them in a few evenings working at home." Many of the endless details were comprised of this type of minutiae, and we used our ingenuity to cover all the bases.

"Andy, with our increased numbers, where will we get enough chairs for the spaghetti dinner tent?" Brian, one of the managers was looking for ideas.

"I already have commitments from funeral homes and churches. Churches have offered to lend us tables too. We'll have to line up some people to take Big Red to pick them up the day before the dinner." *Grandma's* owned two trucks, affectionately known as Big Red and Little Red, to handle hauling jobs appropriate to their names. We were receiving offers of help from many business people and volunteers, who called daily offering to pitch in wherever they were needed. We designed Grandma's volunteer tee shirts that were worn with pride by those who put in their time and effort.

The Honeywell group stipulated in our agreement that I travel to Boston with three of the Minneapolis people to meet the timing experts who would bring the tractor-trailer rig containing their equipment to park next to the restaurant and connect to the power source especially prepared for access to Jeno's computer. In May, I

10K race in Boston, May 1981. Minneapolis Honeywell's Rudy Niemic with two other computer experts (at right) on the back of timing trailer, confer with two of the creators of Boston Marathon timing system, prior to bringing it to Duluth in June to time Grandma's Marathon.

met Rudy, my Minneapolis Honeywell contact and two other members of their team at the Minneapolis airport where we boarded a plane for Boston to work with the timing team at a local 10k race. It was a perfect introduction to the system, and created a good rapport with the Boston team.

Throughout the winter, volunteers called to offer their help. I set them up with colored magic markers and boxes of drawstring bags adorned with the marathon logo. They each wrote large numbers on the bags corresponding to those on the runner packets. A different color was used for each thousand bags which were to be left at the starting line by runners. They contained the runners' jackets and other personal property they couldn't carry while running. At one point, someone remarked, "Watch yourself around Donna or she'll mark you with a registration number and a color code."

Trucks at the starting line loaded the color-coded bags as fast as they were dropped and started back to Canal Park ahead of the runners. Volunteers waited at a grassy field near the finish area to unload the bags in rainbow rows of color (a thousand bags per row) and watch over them until they were retrieved by the triumphant finishers.

On the morning before Grandma's Fourth Marathon, over one-hundred sturdy cardboard boxes containing the runner packets were hauled from a vacant space in the Jeno's building, where I had arranged to assemble them. Across Lake Avenue they came on a parade of two wheelers, dodging traffic to the Aerial Bridge, then into the big tent in Grandma's parking lot. They were arranged by color code on tables around the tent to await the arrival of runners to check in. I stayed to work with the volunteers in the tent to oversee the pickup of packets and solve problems.

On a typical marathon day, I rose at 3:00 a.m., showered, and collected everything I would need for the next eighteen hours. Driving on dark deserted streets, soon to be teeming with spectators, to Lakeside Bakery where I picked up my order from the sleepy baker, I felt calm and satisfied that we were well-prepared. The baker had fresh pastries waiting for my breakfast with the Honeywell team. At that hour, few people were visible when I reached Canal Park. I moved into my parking spot, where my car would stay until long after the race was over. The smell of fresh coffee from Grandma's was welcoming—the kitchen crew had survived the spaghetti dinner and was on board to start the big day. My Honeywell friends came to attention at the smell of fresh pastries, and in the lull of early morning, we had a congenial breakfast before moving into the trailer crammed with computer terminals, scanning wands, printers and paper. Our purpose in rising "with the chickens" was to go over any suspected discrepancies in registrations or last minute changes that always seemed necessary. Timing was the essence of the race and it had to be flawless.

Minneapolis Honeywell employee Jon, Donna, and Grandma's I Manager Debbie wait for early Grandma's Marathon timing results, ca. 1980.

Satisfied that we had everything in order, I boarded a police car with Debbie, Grandma's manager, and headed to the starting line, checking on the aid stations and placement of emergency vehicles as we drove to the banner above the starting line, the last four eyes to view the twenty-six mile course for possible slip-ups before race time. Volunteers were already loading bags, according to color code, onto trucks for the drive back to Canal Park before the starting gun sounded at 9:00 am and thousands of runners surged forward onto the Old North Shore Road. I was in my element. I loved team sports, and this was the biggest team

124

I had ever worked with. The number of participants could only be estimated, considering the citizens of the community who had taken it to their hearts as a matter of community pride.

Along the race course, north shore residents were setting up tables and chairs in preparation to cheer on the first racers as they passed their homes. A calm Lake Superior greeted us as we rode ahead of the runners back to the finish line. They were soon far behind us as we sped to the city where there was much left to be done. Results were to be posted soon after the first runners came in, and would be added until the last runner crossed the line.

Crowds along First Avenue East strained against barriers to catch a glimpse of the first runners to appear on that final stretch of the course. They were torn between wanting to be far enough down the avenue to spot the first competitors, and wanting to be close enough to the finish to see the first one to cross the line. Communications from down the course were being passed along with great excitement. When the first runners appeared, the enthusiastic approval of the crowd buoyed them over the last grueling moments of the finish. As the numbers of finishers increased, there were signs of distress among them, and the medical tent volunteers were kept busy for the remainder of the race.

The timing was underway and running smoothly. For the first time, competitors had quick access to their standings which were posted near the finish line. I began to follow up on details for the awards ceremony to be held in late afternoon.

In the evening there would be beer and dancing in the big tent for those of us who had a second wind at that point. I was amazed at the number of not-so-young runners who were dancing at 10:00 p.m. after running their twenty-six mile race. Tomorrow there would be cleanup throughout the city streets and Canal Park—on Monday morning at the staff meeting we'd begin preparations for next year's race by comparing notes on what went right and what needed improvement. But tonight was to celebrate the triumph for the planners, volunteers, spectators, and most of all—the runners.

When the fourth marathon was over, and *Grandma's II* construction started, Jim approached me about learning shorthand.

"Nobody teaches it anymore, and I really want to learn. I know you can teach me."

"Jim, I'm not a teacher, and I can't even remember how my teacher started us out. I'd like to help you, but I don't have a teacher's manual or even my old Gregg textbook. You can be a great secretary using Dictaphone. Jeno's attorney prefers taping his work, as most executives do today.

Undaunted, Jim said, "But Donna, I have a Gregg text. I found it in a used bookstore. I know you can do it."

It was hard to resist his eager pleas. "Well—bring the book to work, and I'll have a look at it."

The next morning, Jim showed up with the familiar two-toned green Gregg Shorthand book which he wordlessly placed on my desk. I opened it, and was transported back to Miss Golding's classroom. Her teaching came back as if I had never been away.

When Jim had come to me for help, I could barely recall the background of this language learned so many years earlier. Recently, I began writing Jim's story, and turned to the internet to refresh in my mind the history of shorthand. I found the following reminders of its early usage:

In mid-nineteenth century England, when Isaac Pitman invented his "Stenographic Sound" shorthand, he didn't expect it to be confined to office use. He envisioned it becoming a self-contained method of writing that could replace the alphabets of his day. Books written in shorthand appeared in libraries and, over the years, shorthand was adjusted many times to increase speed. This finally made it so difficult to learn that books written in shorthand began to languish on library shelves unread. Some of them still exist, but only as curiosities stored in library basements.

126

Pitman continued to be the most popular method of shorthand in England until the 1980s when the use of shorthand fell off. In America, other methods of shorthand were coming into use, most of them based on the Pitman method. The confusion of styles paved the way for John Gregg to introduce his new method, which was widely accepted and was the shorthand most used in America until it too faded out in the 1980s.

Late in the nineteenth century typewriters were operated by men, office work being considered inappropriate for women. Then by the turn of the century attitudes changed. It was deemed unsuitable for able-bodied men to sit in offices taking shorthand, and was determined to be "respectable" work for women. By 1910, according to the US census that year, eighty-one percent of typists were women, which now was determined acceptable work for a woman.

In my years of office experience, I met some men who had been clerks at the DM&IR Railroad in the days before women in the Duluth community were employed in offices. These men had retained an excellent command of Gregg shorthand, a skill they had not used for thirty years. I usually discovered their knowledge of Gregg when, to my surprise, they couldn't resist looking over my shoulder as I worked, playfully reading aloud from my shorthand notebook.

When the 1980s arrived, it appeared that a major asset in my experience was rapidly finding its way to threatened extinction. Most shorthand notebooks of the secretaries I knew had been replaced by Dictaphones. I had wondered if shorthand was being taught anymore and now, to my amazement, I was taking on an instructor's role at a time when shorthand seemed to have outlived its usefulness.

Jim was worth the investment of time, even though very few employers dictated work to secretaries anymore. Yet, it was the least I could do considering the workload he carried throughout Grandma's Marathon registration.

Jim had watched me use shorthand for other purposes and was convinced it was the key to secretarial success. He believed he had the capacity to develop that skill to achieve his ambition—I agreed, and so our determination to teach Jim this unique skill began that day.

He practiced diligently at home and made rapid progress. I was spending most weekdays in Minneapolis where we were developing *Grandma's II.* On Monday mornings before I left town, I gathered up my correspondence and other work to be completed and carried it with me. Instead of typing my own letters as I usually did because it was more efficient, I called the office in Duluth and dictated to Jim all work that didn't require immediate attention. He postdated and transcribed it. I wanted him to become comfortable working by telephone since that was often the way our people worked. He saved the work until Friday when I came back and looked it over before I signed and sent it off. Meanwhile, Jim was assigned to serve as Andy's secretary, and Andy dictated work to him, adding to his experience. This went on for a few months, and none of his work had to be retyped; this kid was amazing! He had learned to take shorthand notes and transcribe them accurately, and managed it all with a working wife and baby son to help care for. I was proud of his accomplishment.

I had told him the final exam would be held when he was confident enough to take dictation from the Falcon, Jeno's jet aircraft (a tricky process which sometimes included static on the line making it necessary to terminate the call). The conversations often went something like this:

"Can you take a memo for Bob?—over."

"Yes, I'm ready—over" static...

"Can you hear me?" laughter..."Are you getting a little static?—over" static...

"Jeno, I think you're out of range—over" static...

"I'll call in later"—more laughter—"over and out" static...

If Jeno's secretary was out, I usually answered his phone because it was inevitable that the call would involve heavy dictation; and she and I were the only ones in the office who knew shorthand. But that was about to change. The opportunity soon arose for Jim to take his "finals." Jeno's secretary was out—and when the phone rang, Jeno's line lit up. I knew he was on his way to Florida, and this would be a call from the air. I picked up the phone, and when I heard the familiar radiophone noises, I nodded to Jim. He went ahead and answered the call, "Good morning, Jeno—this is Jim—no, he isn't in." His voice was alert and confident. For Jim, a lot was riding on this call—and he knew it. I quietly stayed on the line, as Jim continued.

"Can I take a message for him?"

There was a laugh on the line, and a surprised Jeno said, "Do you take shorthand, Jim?"

"I do—Donna taught me—I'm ready," Jim replied, and within a few seconds began to write furiously in his shorthand book. Those two words, "I'm ready," held a world of late nights poring over a Gregg shorthand text and countless phone calls from Minneapolis for dictation sessions. He was the youngest person I knew who was skilled in shorthand. Due to his determination, under my untrained teaching, he had become a full-fledged private secretary, competent in Gregg shorthand. I stayed on the line simultaneously taking backup notes. He passed his finals easily, and if I had had a laurel wreath, I would have placed it on his golden curls. When Jeno moved his headquarters to Florida in 1984, he took Jim along to work for him.

Grandma's II

During most of the early spring of 1981 I could be found on Washington Avenue in Minneapolis as *Grandma's Inc.* began development of our second restaurant. Mick Paulucci, the owner of *Grandma's*; the president, Andy Borg; the chef, Glenn D'Amour; and me as the office administrator were among the first *Grandma's, Inc.* people on the scene. The others were new to us: architects, contractors, designers, and engineers, determining how to convert the historical site to the restaurant Mick envisioned. My contribution was organization, keeping track of everything, trouble shooting, applying for licensing to sell food and liquor, getting the offices set up—administrative details. We were the ground-breakers paving the way for managers to come on board and begin interviewing employee prospects and preparing for training.

In those early days, before the office was set up, we worked with brief cases, notebooks, clipboards, and accordion files, nomads moving from place to place in the dusty old building staying out of the workers' way. My strategy was to use an indexed loose leaf notebook to keep categorized information at my fingertips. When the notebook became unwieldy, I began transferring pieces to an accordion file (easy to carry around). By the time we could access the third floor to set up the offices, it would be easy to establish permanent records in file cabinets.

In the weeks that followed, I spent hours sitting with the general manager, floor manager, bar manager, chef, and kitchen manager, asking questions about the functions of their departments, taking notes to create training manuals for hostesses, servers, bussers, bartenders, barbacks, and cashiers in front of the house, and line cooks, prep cooks, and dishwashers behind the scenes. I worked with the controller to decide how the two office workers' duties should be meted out and ordering furnishings for the third floor office space.

Grandma's II,
Minneapolis,
1987.

Located on the West Bank at Seven Corners, *Grandma's II* was to be remodeled with a bar and dining room on the main floor and a bar and game room on the lower level. Early in the renovation, a special room was built in the middle of the third floor to house a stained glass dome crafted by a contemporary California artist. The space was designed with a roof skylight for daytime lighting; artificial lights were installed for night to create a dramatic ceiling feature for the pleasure of patrons in the dining room below. The dome was one of many architectural pieces Mick had collected as part of his plan when he began *Grandma's I* in Duluth. These treasures had been carefully photographed, catalogued, and warehoused in Duluth for use in additional restaurants.

Grandma's II was an exciting project, not only for our staff, but the numerous building crews who installed walls, ceilings, electrical and plumbing fixtures, and floors. Tradespeople who worked on the project enjoyed the luxury of having the best materials and equipment to work with. It gave them extra incentive to create a showplace they could be proud to have had a part in building. The artisans who installed the elaborate antique pieces were up to the challenges their inclusion presented.

The antique back-bar, in its heyday, had been the showpiece in the salon of a huge Italian yacht owned by a shipping magnate. The base was composed of mahogany topped with deep green marble; the upper back-bar featured intricately carved shelves highlighted by beveled mirrors. The carpenter who took on the challenge of creating a front bar to live up the its magnificence, matched the mahogany perfectly. A green marble bar top was added to complete the masterful restoration. With matching bar stools upholstered in fabric echoing the rich green marble, the bar became the focal point of the first floor.

Doors at either end of the bar led to kitchen and service areas. They were encased in arched, heavily carved, mahogany frames that had formerly graced the Hollywood home of Jack

Warner. When he rebuilt his home, they were offered for sale and found this new home as a complement to *Grandma's II* elegant bar.

We were a block away from the University of Minnesota Law School Library, and we got our daily exercise by frequent walks to use its Xerox for photocopying until we had access to our own office space. My brain-picking sessions with managers continued, and I prepared training manuals as they alternately interviewed prospective employees. I followed up on licensing for liquor sales, food service, and we all met with health department officials, where I took copious notes to include in manuals for ongoing training. The fire department also had regulations on installing extinguishers and follow-up checking and maintenance.

During the week, we managed our Duluth jobs by telephone, (cell phones and personal computers were still a heartbeat away from reality). Paperwork was carried between the Duluth office and the Minneapolis site by any managers who happened to be coming or going until Fridays when we all returned to Duluth. Monday morning we were back to Minneapolis.

Cash registers were installed that would later be compatible with computer service. We were on the threshold of controlling inventory, purchasing, and payroll with one system located at *Grandma's, Inc.* home office. The management people attended classes with the newly hired restaurant staff to learn the register system. We all needed to use it to provide training and help for the servers and cashiers who would work the system now and later as new people were hired.

Determined to set up scheduling of equipment and building maintenance *before* we opened, I took on the task of collecting all warranty information and manuals from the equipment being installed everywhere in the building. The installers, who needed the instructions to set up the equipment, had an unfortunate habit of leaving the manuals wherever they happened to finish their work. Often I found them on the floor among the debris. I was arranging a schedule with our maintenance manager to avoid falling into a "crisis management" method of dealing with upkeep.

We were well-prepared for the introductory employee meeting, held in midsummer. Our efforts to approach this crucial presentation paid off handsomely—the training program was launched without a hitch.

What would the servers wear in the elegant showplace evolving on Washington Avenue? After much consideration, *Merona* brand jersey

Glenn D'Amour, Grandma's Inc. Executive Chef, ca. 1982.

shirts were chosen in assorted jewel colors, long sleeved and white collared, showing the *Grandma's* logo on the shoulder, to be worn with black pants. With the delivery of the *Meronas,* the third floor space doubled as a dressing room burgeoning with rolling racks of *Merona* rainbows in various sizes. Dressed in royal blue *Merona,* I donned the hat of wardrobe mistress, assisting in selections of suitable colors for our bright, beautiful young people, many of whom attended the nearby University of Minnesota. Additional *Meronas* were ordered for *Grandma's I,* a popular decision with the Duluth staff.

All of the *Grandma's* staff wore the shirts wherever we went in Minneapolis. They evoked questions and interest everywhere, spreading word of the impending opening. This, along with a sign in front of our building and the initial parties that were pending were our only pre-opening promotional plans. I liked this approach of a quiet opening, but many people expressed disagreement with that decision. I heard some rumbling comments that it seemed arrogant to assume the world was waiting, based on hearsay, for the big day.

One day in late summer, when classroom training had

been completed, we scheduled an afternoon hands-on training session for our servers to practice on the newly installed register equipment. We were ready to simulate use of the registers on a dinner shift, followed by end of day check-out procedures.

I went to the supply room for extra register tapes I had ordered, only to discover an empty shelf. I hadn't followed up to ensure the bookkeeper in training had placed the supply order I had given her to be delivered the previous day. It was too late for delivery today, but I had an alternate idea. I told Andy that we were short of register tape and assured him I would have it here in about twenty minutes. He gave me a look that said we needed to talk about the office problem, and I knew we'd have that conversation later.

I hurried out into dazzling August sunshine to Seven Corners turning on Cedar Avenue, where I knew there was a pharmacy, confident that in this university neighborhood they would stock office and school supplies. Moving rapidly, I inwardly laughed at the job envy expressed by some of my acquaintances, who saw my job at *Grandma's* as exciting and glamorous. They should see me now, scurrying down Cedar on my mundane errand. I loved my job, but like all stimulating work, it also exacted hands-on problem-solving. I thought about the pleasant, but clueless office employee who assured me she would restock the supplies. We needed people we could depend on in our fast-paced business, and this was just one more of a growing list of indications that she would not make it past the thirty day trial period. Damn, I hated letting people go!

I refocused my thoughts on the mission at hand, luxuriating in the warm sun. I was about a block from my destination, when a knot of young men appeared, blocking the sidewalk just ahead of me. Because they seemed intent on their conversation, I continued walking expecting they would allow me to pass. I was a few yards from them when I caught the menacing glint of sunlight on a steel knife-blade. It was a surreal moment in that brilliant sunshine on a busy street. Beneath the sun on my shoulders, my blood ran cold, and my immediate instinct was to flee—but where to go? Did the wielder of the blade intend to cut the strap of my purse and snatch it? I avoided eye contact, keeping my eye on the knife. Think...FAST.

Traffic was bumper to bumper, and with no other apparent option, I didn't miss a step as I slipped into the street putting a parked car between us. I sidled quickly past them hugging the sides of two more parked cars before I returned to the sidewalk. Ironically I had observed with relief, as I passed them, that the threat was not directed to me but at one of the young men. Probably a drug deal gone wrong. I didn't stop to find out if anyone was injured. By the time I returned to that spot minutes later, triumphantly clutching my loot from the cleaned-out pharmacy shelf of register tape, all was quiet and there was no blood on the sidewalk.

Safely back at *Grandma's*, Andy asked anxiously: "Did you find some?"

I gave over my bagful of precious register tape.

"I apologize, Andy. It's my job to see that office supply levels are maintained."

Characteristically unruffled, Andy replied, "I'm just glad you had a quick solution. I know you'll sort out the office problem."

Opening parties were a week away. Before they began, however, we would have our own private party for the restaurant staff to enjoy ordering from the dinner menu, prepared by the chef, but served by the managers of *Grandma's, Inc.* staff. Our service was expected to set an example for the new employees and, since I had created the training manuals, I was nervous about practicing what I preached—I had never worked in a restaurant. Mother taught me the rudiments of serving, but that didn't include juggling large trays of cocktails and plated dinners in a busy restaurant. I quickly put in my bid for a table-bussing job, and began to avidly peruse the *Grandma's Bussing Manual.*

Grandma's II opened for lunch on a sunny day near the end of summer. The opening parties had gone well, and the guests were impressed with the decor, the food, and our staff. We had time to pause and smooth out the timing of certain menu items, and traffic from kitchen to dining areas; hostesses and servers had time to get past opening jitters. All of Grandma's staff from management to servers had been given invitations to offer to people of our choice. In addition, people who had worked on the building were invited to the first party.

My daughter Dawn was married to John and living in Minneapolis when the new restaurant was built. It had been a good opportunity to spend time with them. I used my guest tickets to invite them and John's parents to one of the opening parties. The new employees were at their best, and I was proud to have some of my family there to witness our success.

When we looked down Washington Avenue at 11:00 a.m. on the day we officially opened, the question about lack of preliminary advertising was answered. The sidewalk was lined with people waiting for the doors to open. It was an hour early, and Mick said. "Let's open the doors, register guests for tables, and invite them in. It will give them a chance to look around the restaurant before they are seated."

The guests loved this welcoming gesture, and poured into the immaculate setting, where every detail was attended to down to the low flower arrangements by Bachman's on each table.

When I began working in banks, job related travel was not necessary. Now about fifteen years later, I had spent most weekdays through the summer working in Minneapolis. This was not a new concept for me; when I was in junior high, my sister had been sent to Minneapolis by her employer, Northwestern Bell. She was being trained for promotion based on performance and testing. Northwestern Bell was known for their employee training program and promotion of women.

But to some women, it was still unacceptable to leave the city without the protection of a husband. I learned this when an acquaintance invited us to dinner and a bridge game.

When I told her I would be working out of town that

day, she gasped, "Does Hartley *let* you work out of town? Do you travel with *men*. John would *never* allow that!"

I found her tone and questions vaguely insulting. Refraining from informing her what I would like to tell John he could do, I made a mental note to erase them from our social contacts in the future.

I continued to travel to Minneapolis through the winter, although less frequently. *Grandma's II* downstairs bar was in the process of completion, and we had some trouble-shooting to cope with as happens with any new business.

Grandma's II was sold in 2008, and finally closed after serving the Twin Cities community for twenty-seven years. The part I played in the creation of this unusual addition to the list of places to dine in Minneapolis was not only gratifying, but invaluable experience to me in ways I wouldn't realize until some years later.

Mick would create other restaurants in years to come, but before that, an unusual idea was offered to *Grandma's, Inc.* by the Duluth Bayfront Park promotional group. Canal Park and the waterfront area were enjoying a new life with conversion of many old industrial sites into specialty shops and restaurants, attracting tourists to our *Air Conditioned City* in greater numbers than ever before. The Bayfront organization had acquired the old *Flame* restaurant building on the waterfront, and were preparing to reopen it after restoring it to its former glory. *Grandma's, Inc.* with the success of the elegant Minneapolis location, seemed a good corporation to accomplish this.

The Flame to be reopened by Grandma's for Bayfront Group owners.

So the *Flame* became the next restaurant project. *Grandma's, Inc.* would oversee the renovation, provide the staff, and direct the operation after completion of the restoration. We aimed to bring back the elegance of the old *Flame* which had been the epitome of fine dining in Duluth since the 1940s.

The exotic restaurant on London Road owned by Jimmy Oreck was destroyed by fire in 1942 and was reopened in a renovated warehouse building on the waterfront and eventually was restored to its former opulence. The business was sold in 1971 and operated under a couple of owners and renters until it closed in 1982, when Grandma's endeavored to return it to the showplace it had been.

This was a change from the *Grandma's* restaurant format, and we went through the process of style adjustment. We had the advantage of working in our hometown, which cut out travel time and acclimation to a different city. Although most of *Grandma's* employees were too young to remember the *Flame*, I was old enough to have visited the swank supper club on the waterfront location, as a place to celebrate special occasions.

The waterfront *Flame* had been designed in Art Deco style, and we chose to regain that flavor. The maitre d' from the former *Flame*, who still lived in Duluth, gave us helpful information regarding the decor and service of the old restaurant. China, menus, and photos remaining in the building provided additional details. We repeated the preparation and training procedures recently applied to *Grandma's II*, incorporating the

Donna and Hartley with his parents at Flame grand opening, 1983.

style elements of the old *Flame*, including a maitre d' in a tuxedo, who managed the reservation book.

A Minneapolis design firm was hired to decorate the newly remodeled restaurant. Furnishings were special ordered in jewel colors of hot pink and seafoam velvet, and large urns of floral decorations graced every available surface between the large pillars. At the parties preceding the official opening, roving photographers moved through the dining room taking complimentary commemorative photos of the invited guests,

This last attempt to return the *Flame* to its former glory was short-lived. The day had passed where visitors to the city wanted to change from sportswear to dressier clothing for dinner. They liked to go directly from a boat tour or a shopping trip in Canal Park to a more casual dining atmosphere. The *Flame* had opened in September of 1983, and local patrons were not rushing to have dinner at the waterfront during the winter months. Shortly after completing the *Flame* project, *Paulucci Enterprises* moved its headquarters to Florida where Jeno began new business developments. The *Flame* closed within eighteen months after it reopened. *Grandma's I* management people continued to work in the Duluth restaurants, and the City of Duluth took control of Grandma's Marathon.

With my job at *Enterprises* over, it was time to reinvent myself once again.

Flame demolition in preparation for the building of the Duluth Aquarium, ca. 1990.

PART EIGHT

A CORNER STORE

The Plan

In 1985, an inevitable change occurred in my personal world. Twenty-five years of type II diabetes symptoms caught up with Hartley. At age fifty-four he was too young to retire, but unable to continue working as an electrician. We agreed to look for a business that would accommodate his physical limitations.

One Saturday he came home after a round of golf calling out, "I think I've found a place to invest in!" I ran downstairs to hear the details.

"You know Bobby Carl buys properties for Murphy Oil—well, he has just closed a deal for a location that looks like a winner." Murphy Oil, a corporation based in Eldorado, Arkansas, Bobby's hometown, leased properties to entrepreneurs interested in convenience store ownership.

"Bobby said we can lease it if we're interested. I would need your help to manage it—you have the business experience to help put it together. I know it's asking a lot, but I hope you'll consider it."

"It could be a viable business for any community, like a corner store—everyone needs gas and groceries, and I'd like to make money for ourselves instead of other people for a change. Tell me the details and we can look at the prospects."

It was the last thing I would have chosen to do; I had no retail sales experience—had never used a cash register except to train others, and didn't even like shopping. Hartley liked grocery shopping, and was always willing to take on that chore during my working days. I knew I'd have to get behind the counter and face customers to be effective in employee training. I believed that unless we experienced the daily duties expected of our employees, we could not know if our expectations were reasonable. It would take at least a year of working various shifts for me to see what problems each season brought.

It was unlikely that Hartley would find a better opportunity to prepare for retirement, and I had found that business was business. I could use my creativity to discern the needs of our customers and devise ways to meet them. After mulling over these ideas carefully, I would support Hartley and give it my best effort if we agreed, after creating a business plan, that this golden opportunity was as viable an opportunity as it appeared to be.

The property was located on a corner in the midst of a small business district at the busy intersection of Fourth Street and Sixth Avenue East. St. Mary's and St. Luke's, the two largest hospitals in Duluth were located a few blocks east and west of the store. It was a perfect place for hospital staff, who worked day or night shifts, summer and winter, to stop for gas and a gallon of milk on the way to and from work. The building housed an oil change business before Murphy took possession, giving us an opportunity to watch the traffic flow patterns from our car parked near the driveways. We drove in and out of the three driveways at various times of day to test accessibility to the property. Studying demographics and competition, we were convinced we would need to stay open twenty-four hours a day if we hoped to build a solid market share. Our plan was to maintain that schedule as long as we could at least break even on the night shift. If the night shift lost money, we might reconsider shorter hours.

Preparation

I called my former boss, Bob Heller, who had generously offered to help anytime I needed an attorney. He had moved to the University of Minnesota where he headed the Small Business School for entrepreneurs to obtain advice and education in launching small business operations. He also continued to do some legal work for friends. We had worked together on small business investments, and it was like going back in time, only now the investment was Hartley's and mine.

I had learned from working with Bob not to negotiate any contract (large or small) without legal consultation. Bob examined the proposed lease, and suggested a few adjustments. He recommended that we incorporate the business to protect us in case it failed, and was obliged to advise us of the percentage of small businesses that fail in the first year, a depressing prospect to contemplate. I had been confident to this point, in spite of an economic slump that was not the best climate in which to open a business. Bob, seeing my crestfallen look, laughed and said. "You aren't going to fail. I've worked with you long enough to be sure of that, but it's my job to advise you of the pitfalls."

I was mollified as he offered his blessings, one of a few as it turned out. Most of our acquaintances, except for friends who operated businesses of their own, were doubtful, horrified to think of starting a business during an economic slump. Those who supported us admitted it was hard work, but worth it. They offered whatever help they could give, and were encouraging. I began to be excited at the prospect of a chance to put some of my own ideas into practice.

There had been times when I cursed my money-handling affinity that had led to being assigned roles requiring accountability for large sums. I often disagreed with management's business philosophy in the past, but my opinions rarely prevailed in practice. This was an opportunity to put financial planning together with my theories to work for us. The size of the business was of less concern to me than achieving optimum results—customer satisfaction and healthy net profit.

I believed the first step to develop a good customer base was to take a cue from the needs of customers rather than thinking they'd take whatever we offered and like it. I had been given a chance to train employees and saw that good results came from letting them know their job was vital to the success of the business. If we didn't treat their work as significant, we could hardly expect them to give it their best effort. Luckily, Hartley agreed with me, and we also agreed if we couldn't succeed without cheating on taxes, customers, employees or suppliers, we didn't belong in business. Time would tell if our high-flown ideas were realistic.

Hartley called Bobby Carl to accept the offer and we arranged financing. We personally financed the purchase of equipment and merchandise to stock the shelves. This is not the sort of investment that banks are interested in backing. They need viable collateral, not gas in the ground or stock on shelves. In June with a target date of Labor Day weekend for opening, we signed the lease, and Hartley retired officially, a requirement to obtain an annuity held in trust and earmarked for our initial investment. Our bridges were burned—we were committed for better or worse to the course we had charted.

With three months until completion of the building, we selected vendors, applied for licenses, set up accounts for withholding and other taxes, banking, arranged for utilities, and made equipment selections. My previous business experience and Hartley's strong math background, his knowledge of everything related to the building, its maintenance, and city code requirements made for a good combined effort.

I took on preparing an initial order to stock shelves and Hartley contacted beverage vendors to plan for filling the wall of coolers that were incorporated into the building specs. He also ordered snack foods and planned a menu of deli items we intended to offer.

Under Control

Then, in the middle of a July night, the unthinkable happened. Our home was invaded by a rapist who attacked me while I slept fitfully in my living room. I had strained my back and, uncomfortable in bed, I had come downstairs to watch an old TV movie, hoping to drift off to sleep on the comfortable sofa. I was awakened when my breathing was cut off. I struggled to get free of whatever was covering my face, and saw a stocking-headed figure bending over me with a cloth that exuded a pungent odor pressed against my face. Terrified, I fought my lonely losing battle—I had already inhaled enough of the substance, which I concluded was chloroform, to knock me out. I awoke on the floor of the living room, discarded there by my attacker with my hands bound. I easily slipped my hands from the binding, which was an odd cotton knee-high stocking.

Hartley had not awakened...I could hear the air conditioner humming from the bedroom where he slept above me. Afraid to move, I crouched by the fireplace until I was sure the intruder was gone, and then ran for the stairs and into the bedroom to wake Hartley. The police came quickly in answer to his call, bringing a canine unit to see if a scent could be picked up, but to no avail. They took me to the hospital, and in the next few hours detectives began their business of questioning.

It was a separate and painful event—there is no need to dwell on it here. I include it in this story only as a commentary on the effect it had on an already stressful time in our lives— and as witness to the resilience of the human spirit to prevail over impossible circumstances. Buoyed by the strength of Hartley, our family, and many friends, I was determined not to let a pathetic random criminal act define my future. I would take back control.

I was heartsick that the trauma left me with a temporary inability to concentrate. I had worked for other people getting their businesses started, and it was painfully ironic that I was unable to give the same energy and attention to our own. I needed to be at my best to accomplish all that had to be done, and I fought to keep my focus on the details of our preparations. If nothing else, necessity motivated the intensity of my effort and seemed to hasten the healing process. Gradually the ability to concentrate on my work improved.

During this period, Dawn had graduated from St. Catherine's and made the decision to apply to William Mitchell College of Law in St. Paul. She continued her job at AT&T while attending school, and came to Duluth every weekend, laden with law books, to be with me. I could not change her mind, she remained steadfast in her determination to see me through until the store opened. We worked side by side, she on her studying and me on my endless lists of merchandise.

Deadline Respite

Although eroding our capital funding, it was almost a welcome respite when construction delays put off our opening until mid-December, extending my recovery period and giving us time to complete our plans. Some of the excitement of putting our own ideas into practice returned. It was important that we make good decisions about policy, procedures, and employee training and put them into place before we opened our doors. My enthusiasm for the project slowly returned during that shaky start toward recovery. My experience working on Grandma's restaurant openings gave me some good parallels to work from; liquor license vs beer license, stocking packaged and canned foods vs fresh food. Coolers, freezers, cash register equipment, deli foods were all much the same as for restaurant use. We agreed that equipment used by employees should be top quality (registers, calculators, and accessories). They were the lifelines in a retail store, and their failure could create a minor disaster in a twenty-four hour a day operation.

We were aware that wholesale prices were not friendly to small stores, but it was a shock to learn the discrepancy between prices offered supermarkets and convenience stores. Larger retail businesses sold many items for less than we could buy them at wholesale, so Hartley and I went on several large shopping trips, paying close attention to the expiration date on each item. We filled the alcove in our living room, blocking off my piano with bags of canned goods for which we paid less at retail than our supplier would charge. Access to the piano was of little concern in the face of our concentration on the task at hand—I couldn't recall the last time I had played it.

Hiring had been accomplished shortly after we made the decision to buy the business. We had no trouble finding workers to cover the three eight-hour shifts we planned to schedule. We bought extra drawers for the cash register, and I sewed bags from sturdy denim and Velcro, labelled with shift numbers to hold the currency and coin each employee needed for opening tills. At the end of their shift, they removed the till to count its contents and prepare an accounting sheet of their shift on which they had recorded their drops of currency in the floor safe. As they removed their till from the register, the employee coming on duty replaced it with an empty till waiting under the counter, quickly counting the money from the denim bag for their shift into the till, and beginning to work.

Hartley and I would start by each working one of the three shifts. We decided the first shift at six in the morning was best for me, and he and my nephew Tom would alternate each week on the two later shifts. Tom was going to take over as manager after we got underway—we needed to begin making money before increasing payroll costs. It might take a year or more before we could afford to pay a manager.

By November, plans and preparation were complete, and we had access to a partially completed building. We were dodging construction workers, but we were pulling it together. We even put up holiday decorations.

Bob Heller called to ask if I would participate in a seminar as part of his Small Business program at UMD. The theme was "How to Operate a Small Business Successfully." Taken aback, I said. "Bob, we aren't open yet—I can hardly declare us successful."

He chuckled before answering, "You'll succeed, don't worry. You have taken all the right steps. All you need to do for the talk at UMD is tell people contemplating small business investment the steps you took in making the decision and how you made preparations to begin operating your business."

The building was still in the finishing stages, so I agreed, and prepared my speech. On a cold evening in November, I presented myself at UMD to give my talk. It was one of the first times I ventured out alone at night since I had been attacked, and it took all my courage to get into my car in the dark. Once underway, it was fun to compare notes and work with the other two owners of diverse small businesses, and I saw people I knew who represented insurance, advertising, and other services for aspiring business owners to consider. Participation in this workshop gave me back some of my confidence, and I believed Bob was right—we would not fail.

The Reality

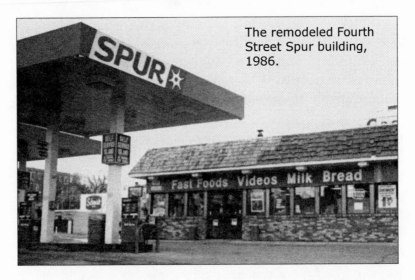

The remodeled Fourth Street Spur building, 1986.

Construction was near completion by Thanksgiving and we planned a mid-December opening. The weeks of investment with no return had stretched out to three months longer than planned. Yet we were determined that the store would be fully stocked with everything in place before the doors opened.

We began stocking the shelves, jockeying for position among tile installers and electricians. We resisted pressure from the lessor to start selling from the full gas tanks. We were not responsible for the delay and it was worth waiting a little longer to open our door with a full inventory to serve customers well and encourage their return.

Studies by Murphy Oil before acquiring the building had estimated high gas sales and lower inside sales. Hartley and I had lived in Duluth most of our lives. We knew the neighborhood and expected high inside sales, and we would be well-stocked to take advantage of that potential. Many of the neighborhood residents had no means of transportation and wouldn't buy gas, but we expected their walk-in business to boost overall income. This proved to be the case—inside sales far exceeded even our expectations.

The winter of 1985-86 was bitter, with heavy snowfall. It was minus twelve degrees when we opened on December 12, with Tom on the night shift. After a night of fitful sleep, I drove out in the 5:30 a.m. icy darkness to reluctantly face my first day. Tom reported brisk business until 2:00 a.m. giving him time to restock and clean before I arrived. I was encouraged, but scared. I confessed to Tom that I was daunted by the prospect of working behind the counter. I felt far out of my element, standing in the well-lit front window—alone in a fishbowl of alien waters. Tom was reluctant to leave me there. He said, "I'll stick the tanks before I go." He went to the back room for the eight foot stick that measured the remaining gas in two underground tanks. Running out of gas was the cardinal sin in this business, so "sticking the tanks" was a critical function to measure supplies before the beginning shift. It was also my least favorite chore, particularly on windy days when I teetered like a drunken tightrope walker clutching my flailing balance pole as I struggled toward the tank covers. The small tank covers were removed from the ground and the unwieldy stick lowered into the tanks. Markings etched along its length reached to the very bottom of the tanks, marking the amount of remaining fuel by a darkening of the varnished wood where the wetness of gas began. When he finished, I told Tom to leave. After all, he had to be back at 10:00 p.m. to work through the next night.

I couldn't believe I was terrified in these surroundings I had had a large part in creating, but I somehow managed a welcoming smile and greeting when my first customer appeared. He was more interested in looking over the store and asking questions about it than in assessing my qualifications. He made complimentary comments on the appearance of the store and noting the sign naming Hartley as the lessee asked: "Is this a locally owned store?"

"Yes my husband and I own the business."

"I will be coming here regularly—I like supporting people who invest their money in community businesses."

More people arrived, and soon I was too busy to worry about my lack of cashiering experience. Before I knew it, from our location above the water, I saw the sun rising rosy red over a frosty, steaming Lake Superior heralding the new day, and my spirits lifted. Many of those first visitors became loyal customers through the twelve years we owned the business.

Skyworld publication pictures Donna and Hartley after December 1985 opening.

A small neighborhood newspaper had carried a story announcing the opening with Hartley and me pictured in our new building on the front page. It was helpful in attracting interest. In the midst of this Christmas season, immersed in get-

150

ting under way, we were surprised at the volume of sales and the demands of reordering. We received two deliveries a week from our major supplier, and refilled the gas tanks twice a week or more. It hadn't occurred to me that the initial stocking would have to be repeated that frequently. Our lives became a round of reordering and restocking shelves during lulls between customers. I regularly worked long past my own shift when Hartley arrived at 2:00 p.m. to take over the next shift. Hartley, Tom, and I didn't see each other much except in passing. We all had our share of stocking and cleaning—and the customer base kept building.

The ad for the official grand opening in February, 1986.

Christmas arrived, and we scheduled ourselves to work along with the weekend employees on four-hour shifts so everyone had time with their families. We needed to be on duty during the holidays at Fourth Street Spur to know how to prepare for them in the future. After his midday shift, Hartley drove to Minneapolis to pick up our son, who was arriving at the airport

151

from Georgia, and our daughter from her home in the city to drive them to Duluth for Christmas. He planned to arrive at the store to pick me up when Tom arrived to take over at 8:00 p.m. It was the first time I worked alone during evening hours.

I was doing fine until traffic slowed after 6:00 p.m. and the streets cleared as people retired to their homes in the starry Christmas Eve stillness. The building remained deserted, except for me until around 6:30 when a car drove up to the door and screeched to a halt. Three young men emerged and entered the store, jostling each other and laughing loudly. They were obviously under the influence of drugs or alcohol—drugs appeared to be the most likely. One stopped and leaned over the counter leering, "Ooh, are you all alone here?"

A small alarm sounded in the back of my mind. Then one of his companions dragged him over to the junk food racks. They lingered over their selections, speaking in low tones and looking over at me occasionally. They finally brought their purchases to the counter and checked them out. The aggressive one again leaned over the counter, his eyes unfocused. "Maybe I'll stick around for a while to keep you company," he suggested.

We were near the police station, and I thought about picking up the phone, but held back, fearful of exacerbating a potentially dangerous situation. I caught a glimpse of three figures in the driveway heading for the door. They peeked in and asked if they could come in to get warm while they waited for someone who was to pick them up. Hoping my fear didn't show I said, "You must be frozen. Help yourselves to coffee and pastries. You're welcome to stay as long as you like. Someone will be here soon to take over for me, so we won't be closing."

I hoped my unwelcome visitor would get the idea that reinforcements were on the way. It seemed to work—he hastened to the door and got back into the car, but it remained in the driveway near the entrance. A second set of headlights sweeping the driveway, brought a momentary surge of new customer hope, but my heart quickly sank when the threesome waiting for their ride hurried to the door saying, "There's our ride. Merry Christmas—and thanks for the coffee!"

They left the driveway, as the door of the waiting vehicle opened and my tormentor stepped out, ready to come back in. I was fumbling under the counter for the key to the front door, planning to lock him out, but someone had moved the key. When I looked out the window, I was staring into his face as he approached the door. In that moment, the months of rage culminated into a surge of power. I was not the sleeping woman of six months ago, vulnerable to attack in her own living room.

Before he could open the door, I picked up the phone as I continued to look directly into his face. I punched buttons and spoke rapidly into the phone, forming the words distinctly, "He's walking toward the door." The man turned, jumped into the back seat of the car, and it squealed out of the driveway. Now I looked in earnest for the key under the counter. I was still going to lock up for fear they would return.

With key in hand I triumphantly stood up ready to head for the door when, through the window, I saw a smiling Tom walking toward the building, then opening the door. "Merry Christmas, Donna. Mom and I had our dinner early, so I came right down in case Hartley got back before eight."

When I left the store each day, I emptied the floor safe and took the cash home to count and prepare a deposit which I dropped in the night depository at the bank. I held out cash and coin necessary to fill the denim bags for the three starting tills. Then I began my accounting chores, and on weekends prepared payroll and wrote checks for the week's expenses. I was diligent in maintaining my records for the accountant who would prepare our tax return next September at the end of our first fiscal year. It seemed far off, but I knew it would arrive only too soon. I flatly refused to take on the responsibility of preparing and filing tax returns. There was a limit to how much one person could do.

Our main concern in December, the closing of Fourth Street for resurfacing which had blocked off one driveway since it began shortly after we opened, threatened to go on for months. Heavy snows continued throughout the winter, and it seemed our plowing service visited us every few days. The city plows constantly created high banks of snow that required constant unblocking our two remaining driveways. We ran out of room for the snow and had to engage truckers to haul it out. The expense was startling, yet that was why we had a contingency fund, which was dwindling alarmingly. True to their word, at the end of this winter siege, when the street opened, Murphy Oil compensated us for estimated loss of sales. We had squeaked through, and spring finally arrived.

The Staff

Kim was the daughter of a golfer and had worked at the golf course. She also worked at a supermarket, and the job with us supplemented her income. Bill captained the UMD football team and worked nights to help finance his education. Scooter, who also attended UMD was the stepson of another golfer. Keith, who had studied accounting, had been unable to find an accounting job in the prevailing economic slump. The asset of his training was a bonus for us. We had hired these extra people to handle the weekend shifts, so Hartley and I could have the extra thirty-two hours between us to devote to our other duties.

We arranged a Christmas Party at the restaurant next door to the store, and staggered shifts so everyone had a chance to attend. They all had helped get the business started and we wanted to show our appreciation.

There would be many other employees in the months and years to come. Jean and Trudy, who continued to work at the store long after we sold it. We found Al to work every night shift during the week and Jason who worked every Saturday and Sunday night. Cab drivers and police officers stopped frequently during the long night shifts to be sure everything was okay. Cab drivers had radio equipment to summon the police if they found

Bill Dunsmoor, Fourth Street Spur Cashier, at work, ca. 1986.

anything amiss, which was reassuring. Most of the convenience stores in our area had been robbed at least once. The two detectives who had investigated the July attack in our home kept in touch to see how I was doing. They let us know that police were still keeping watch on our home.

Convenience stores around the country were favorite targets of robbers. In many large cities, night cashiers worked from a locked enclosure where customers prepaid for gas. Our well-lighted corner was visible to many residents living on our hillside, and some of them told us they watched the activity on our corner from their windows when they had trouble sleeping. Like sentinels, they were ready to call the police at the least provocation. Despite the deterrents to burglars, I particularly worried about the safety of night shift cashiers. Employees on every shift had been trained to give up the money in the till without resistance, in case of a robbery. Our first concern was for their safety.

The late-evening abduction and murder of a young woman working alone in a Highway 35 convenience store about thirty-five miles away prompted us to hire extra people to augment the weekend shifts. We had never scheduled women at night, even with our highly visible location close to the police department. Week nights were relatively quiet, but weekends brought out a more threatening element, which reflected changes in the neighborhood. It was hard to find quality help to work the night shift, and it represented the fastest turnover of the three shifts.

One month, I received an unusually large phone bill which showed a number of outgoing calls on weekend nights, all to one long distance number, during the same shift on Saturday nights. Taking the most direct route, I simply dialed that number and was appalled to hear a raspy-sounding voice spewing gay porn. Evidently our "extra" Saturday night guy was making late night phone calls as business thinned out, when Jason was out of earshot, busy with side work. This was reflected in the billing which listed a number of thirty-second calls, where he was interrupted by Jason or a pesky customer, and simply kept trying until he could settle down to listen. I prepared the young man's final paycheck and reported my findings to Hartley, who called on him at the store to confront him on his next shift. When he saw Hartley enter the store at 10:00 p.m. the guilty employee knew the jig was up. Not waiting for the axe to fall he asked, "Do you want me to finish my shift?"

Hartley handed him his final check saying, "No, you've already cost us enough, I'll take over."

"I could pay back the money."

At Hartley's reply, "No, just leave," he headed dejectedly for the door.

He was replaced by Jason's Doberman, who sat behind the counter with him. I said nothing, expecting every day to hear from the authorities that the Doberman would have to go, but no one ever questioned his "assistant to the night man" position. Jason was competent to handle the volume of business just fine. The additional person was hired as a bow to the adage: There is safety in numbers. In this case a well-trained Doberman, with no addiction to pornography filled in nicely for the "extra man."

We had to trust our employees who were totally responsible for managing their eight-hour shifts through that first long winter and the twelve years beyond. We had a few who stole from us, which was shortly detected. The thieves couldn't deny their guilt and were let go.

But in 1991, the year of the infamous storm, we discovered just how reliable and loyal our employees were. The storm began innocently enough on Halloween evening with house-holders clucking sympathetically what a shame it was that the little trick-or-treaters' costumes were becoming bedraggled. The storm's mild onset was belied by a record snowfall in its three-day run. For those three days, we were unable to leave our street by car.

We became concerned the first day about employees be-ing stranded at the store, and telephoned the cashier on duty with instructions to lock the doors and take care of the key until we were able to return to business. She told Hartley the staff had already worked out a plan among themselves for those who lived within walking distance to alternate shifts so we could keep the store open and serve the neighborhood while continu-ing to produce income.

The few people who waded through hip-deep drifts to maintain their self-imposed schedule continued to do their accounting for each shift as usual. They made up tills for the person coming on duty and kept their daily account sheets me-ticulously. The first day, Hartley received a call from the cashier who advised him the floor safe was stuffed full. Hartley told him to hide their money drops under the counter and, at the end of their shifts, place them at the bottom of a freezer under the food. He made up a schedule for new hiding places to put the money from each shift and called them in daily.

Manager Peter Jeronimus of North Shore Bank called me on the third day to say he had made it to the bank in his four-wheel drive vehicle and asked if we needed cash or coin to operate the store. The coin was sadly depleted, even though customers paid in coin whenever possible to help the cause. Peter was able to bring all the coin we needed to the store in exchange for currency, but regulations prevented him from tak-ing cash deposits from the store to the bank.

Tom was the first to be freed from the white prison and make his way to Fourth Street Spur, where he placed or-ders to resupply the depleted shelves (gas remained in good supply, since no one had been able to drive). Our employees were neighborhood heros, who had taken care of the needs of anyone who could walk to the store (and our heros for keeping us in business), the only business open for blocks. The orders placed that day were almost as large as our initial order before we started our business.

Tom collected all the money from the freezers, using Hartley's list of ingenious hiding places, and money from every shift was accounted for. When the money bags had run out at the store, the clerks substituted envelopes they took from stock so the accounting was in good order. I waded out to Forty-Fifth Avenue East and Gladstone Street to meet Tom and retrieve a large shopping bag of cash. I dragged it back the half block to our home and began to count money for the largest deposit we would make in our history. It took me until late in the evening to finish. I had had a break from this tedious job for three days, and I knew I would pay the price for my mini-vacation when the storm ended. The next day, I was able to struggle by car to deposit the money in our bank three blocks from home.

After the first year and a half, our employees numbered twelve, and Tom was managing with Hartley visiting the store daily to collaborate with him on operations, while I handled the financial business from my office at home, rarely visiting the store. I had spent about twenty hours a day between working in the store behind the counter, stocking shelves, cleaning, and making up deposits in my home office, taking care of paper-work, and managing a household. It was becoming difficult to sleep, and I realized I was trying to micromanage every part of our lives.

One day, along in our second year of operation, a friend who was also a sales rep for one of our vendors, during a routine business call commented, "Donna, you look like garbage. You need to get out of here!"

A close look in the mirror confirmed Jayne's blunt ob-servation that only a friend could voice, and I saw a person I barely recognized. That day I went home, never to return to my impossible schedule. No, the store wasn't as neat and tidy, and we probably lost some dollars, but I knew that total collapse of either Hartley or I would be disaster. I finally decided to stay home permanently for the sake of my health—physical and emotional. I acknowledged that my presence was not indispensable, and thereafter worked from my home office.

A Wise Decision

Toward the end of our twelfth fiscal year, I was recovering from heart surgery and we were due to renew our three-year lease. Tax time was nearing, which reminded me that it was never my intention to work with money or accounting, yet ironically, much of my work experience had required hands-on control of large sums of money. In our business, I dealt with my dread of tax season by meticulous entry of monthly accounting on a hand-prepared spread sheet to present to John Signorelli, our C.P.A. Fiscal year-end became the harbinger of ominous (although unlikely) possibilities in my mind, and I still did not trust the computer with year-end account reconciliation. I wonder in retrospect how I managed the stress of my unrealistic schedule, yet there was comfort in the accurate figures I confidently presented to John at tax time.

Prompted by the state of my health, I suggested it was time to consider selling the business. Hartley disagreed, but instinct told me another three years might be too stressful for me to handle. We had turned our investment into a thriving business with a three-year lease, wide customer base, and existing inventory to offer prospective buyers. I reminded him that we had managed the business well and accomplished our goal of preparing for our retirement. Hartley reconsidered when I pointed this out and agreed to begin preparations for sale. I called Bob Heller, who drew up a sale contract, agreed that we had priced it realistically, and so we were ready to seek a buyer. Bob noted that small business owners often consider the hours of struggle they devoted to the development of their own place and factor it into their asking price. We hadn't considered our investment beyond just the funding and laughed at the prospect of trying to estimate our hours and exact payment through the sale. Small business owners learn quickly that long hours come with the territory.

Now we reversed the process of opening, and found the sale to be more difficult than starting had been. Finding a buyer was no problem, and we agreed to turn over the business without closing our doors to prevent a break in service to the community. It was what Hartley and I would have liked had we been the buyers, however, it was exacting and difficult to manage. The lesson that stayed with me regarding the need for assistance of a good attorney when entering into contracts paid off during the closing period as well as it had in starting our business. Bob had stressed that, although he had offered a fair contract, he represented our interest in its preparation, and suggested the buyers ask their attorney to review it before signing. They declined this advice. Then, they decided the contract needed changing after it had been signed and the business turned over to them. It was uncomfortable, but the contract was fair, and we held firm.

On our last day of business at the end of April 1997, we stuck the gas tanks before we left the store for the last time, to determine the amount of gas to include for the final inventory. A week later, almost one year after my first heart surgery, I arrived near midnight at St. Mary's urgent care with a ruptured aorta. My instinct to sell had been amazingly accurate, and my survival a medical miracle. Two weeks later, I was released to begin cardiac rehab for the second time.

This hiatus gave me an opportunity to learn something about the younger generation. My grand-niece Shelby worked in my home office with me during her summer high school breaks. She often surprised me with her PC skills, and now I needed her to take over some of the work I never would have asked her to do had I been well. When I returned from the hospital, Shelby had caught up on most of the accounting work, by looking at my records and continuing accordingly.

At home, I viewed the aftermath of the sale, and saw it would be weeks before I could finish the partial year income tax records, pay the remaining bills, close out accounts, and comply with required government paperwork. During that period, I was extremely grateful I had had the foresight to pay vendors on delivery to avoid facing, along with our other closing expenses, a huge amount of outstanding debt, for merchandise long since sold.

The twelve long years of self-employment ended, not with a fanfare, but with a whisper I barely recognized as the end. I had stayed the course that we had agreed would offer us the best opportunity to secure our retirement. It took a little time before I could sigh with relief, breathe deeply, and dare to contemplate my potentially promising future.

Hartley, Jr. at AVP Video Productions in Athens, Georgia, ca. 1986.

Dawn in her law office in Hamburg, Iowa, ca. 1992.

PART NINE

PINNACLES

Aftermath

My retirement didn't begin until age 64 in 1997 when I had cleared up the interminable details related to the sale of our business. During those weeks I also completed the cardiac rehab vital to recovering heart surgery patients. From my experience of the previous summer, I knew recuperation would involve many months. Throughout my hospital stay, Hartley cared for the pots of seedlings I had planted in the sun room in anticipation of having fabulous flower gardens that summer. On my return home, I was touched to see many of them blooming and pictured Hartley faithfully watering them daily. I gave most of them to friends and neighbors as gardening was off-limits to me for the summer. It was an extremely cold spring, yet I sat on a bench in my rose garden wearing a winter jacket, just happy to smell the outdoors—grateful for my life.

In July, the weather warmed and I could sit among the roses and other perennials enjoying the warmth of the sun. The recovery was long as I expected, and I learned that I had had what was termed a "small" stroke during my emergency heart surgery. Usually the symptoms disappear in time, but as I began healing, I found there was some residual damage remaining. It was a small price to pay for my survival. I spent many contemplative days as I slowly began walking on my treadmill in bad weather and outdoors on sunny days, increasing my distance a little each day. I was gaining strength. At the beginning of 1999, my friend Joan Smith, who knew I had written stories and poems since childhood, asked me if I would like to attend a memoir writing class with her.

"Count me in!" I replied, delighted to have an opportunity to finally take the step I needed to structure the stories I had been struggling with. I had vast writing experience during my years in business—some of it creative, but not the same as the life stories I was striving to write for my family. Mara Kirk Hart was our instructor, and the moment I entered her classroom, I felt as if I had struck gold. The focus of my future was settled that day, and Mara became teacher, mentor and lifelong friend to me. I took off with my stories and never looked back. I realized this was what I should have been doing all of my life. I began to learn how to frame the stories I had thrown away in frustration, retrieved them from my memory and rewrote them. I had found this woman's place in the world. I converted the home office I had used for business to "Donna's Study." I set it up to accommodate my books and writing tools.

Lake Superior Writers' Wednesday memoir group formed in 1999. Kay Coventry, Dorothy Lutz, Janice Fontaine, Margaret Kinetz, and Donna, ca. 2010.

On the Threshold of 2000

About the time our business was winding down with the dawning excitement of my new writing life on the horizon, references began to surface about technological problems that might accompany our transition into 2000, the new millennium, which was now simply called Y2K. Could rumors be true that the great minds carrying us into cyberspace had made no provision to move beyond 1999?

John Koskinen, appointed by President Clinton as Special Coordinator of the United States effort in the race to correct this oversight assured us we had every reason to be confident. I was counting on the brilliant mind power and billions of dollars invested in the great Y2K race to prevent major breakdown of computer-controlled services throughout the world. There was worldwide concern that the situation provided a perfect climate for terrorist activities, and every wild-eyed Chicken Little predictably emerged from their coops to declare the end of the world was at hand.

Media hyperbole, fueled by speculation, threatened to create public reaction that could result in shortage of food and other supplies, as well as overloaded communication systems. I began to wonder if perhaps the real race was not between the technology experts and the clock, but between the media glut of hysteria-producing speculation and the ability of the population to remain rational in their thinking and controlled in their actions.

I was happy to see December 31, 1999, dawn with record-setting high temperatures. Media reports were full of news from major world cities sharing their decisions for long-planned celebrations. The United States had the advantage of seeing the new millennium arrive in many world cities before midnight came to our country. Most of the cities had decided to stay with their plans for elaborate exhibitions to welcome in the year 2000. As we watched early newscasts from around the world, we saw spectacular fireworks and impressive pageantry.

A sad note was a report from Kosovo where dark skies were a grim reminder that United Nations troops continued their struggle to maintain their peacekeeping vigil. I stayed awake to see a Times Square teeming with over two million celebrants appearing on our TV screen without incident, and so began the twenty-first century and a new millennium.

New Millennium - New Life

As we returned to the business of everyday living during the new year, many friends and acquaintances asked how I came to write my memoirs. They had looked for classes to attend without success. I decided to design a course for beginning memoir writers. I had never taught, but in my working days, I had created a number of jobs and training materials to go with them for people I interviewed and selected to train for those jobs. I was confident I could parallel that experience, modifying it to teach memoir writing. I outlined a six-week course based on the text Mara used in my beginning class, made copies to present my idea, and called Mara. "Do you think I can do it adequately?"

"Of course," she assured me, and you are welcome to use any handout materials I've prepared for beginning writers."

I planned to volunteer my time to avoid tuition costs so anyone could take advantage of the opportunity to start writing. Mara gave me good advice about tailoring my program to the format I proposed to use, and I contacted the person who approved proposals for small group activities in my large church congregation. She was enthusiastic about the idea, and I offered to send my proposal. In 2000, I taught my first class to a group of twelve with good results. Interest was piqued by word of mouth, and people wanted to know when I would offer another class. I did teach a second class, and the members wanted to continue writing together in a group. I agreed to remain as facilitator, gradually turning over that role to each member in turn, during the next five years.

A Year of Loss

Meanwhile, in 2001, Hartley was ill, and signs of the congestive heart failure that resulted from faulty heart valves plagued me again. I went back to surgery to replace another valve and Hartley was not far behind me for surgery to explore the suspected return of lymphoma, which we had believed was in remission.

On April 14, 2003, our fifty-second wedding anniversary, just after noon, we watched in horror as the interior of our home and its contents were destroyed by fire. It began innocently enough beneath the back deck in a bit of dried grass. The small, flickering flame was quickly betrayed by a wisp of smoke and its smell, but despite prompt response by fire fighters, the greedy flames could not be subdued.

When it was safe to enter the house, the fire fighters managed to locate and salvage my jewelry and two binders of stories. My quick-thinking son, Hartley Jr. retrieved our photo albums, tore the pages from the covers, dried them, and was able to salvage them. My treasured Chickering baby grand piano could not be salvaged, however, and I gave it to my piano tuner to use in restoration of a matching model he was working on. Our remaining belongings, except for family remembrances, could be replaced. For the next few months, we were totally absorbed in locating a new home, replacing our belongings, and dealing with insurance business. We found the home I still occupy in a newly completed apartment building in Lester Park near our former neighborhood.

2C Tuesday, April 15, 2003

MINNESOTA WISCONSIN BRIEFS

DULUTH

Fire consumes Lakeside home

A fire severely damaged a home Monday afternoon in Duluth's Lakeside neighborhood.

B. Hartley and Donna Schilling were in their house, at 4518 Gladstone St., when a neighbor spotted a fire under the deck just after noon, said Assistant Duluth Fire Chief Jim Ray. Preliminarily indications are that the fire started with some outdoor wiring, he said.

The couple was able to get safely out of the 2½-story house as the deck was quickly engulfed. The fire then spread inside, Ray said. He said the fire likely destroyed the home.

He estimated damage at $75,000, but the fire department could push that estimate to more than $100,000 including the personal belongings, Ray said.

Before another year had passed, the loss of our home paled in significance when we discovered that Hartley was losing his battle with lymphoma. It was a dramatic lesson in reassessing perspectives. In his remaining days, Hartley focused his concern on my future, encouraging me to continue my writing and the new friendships I was developing. When he slipped away on the evening of February 26, 2004, at the age of seventy-three, I embarked on a lonely new journey. Although I had known for weeks that his illness was terminal, I was stunned by the awful emptiness of bereavement that overwhelmed me. I found myself asking my children, "What will we do now?" It was hard to believe Hartley was no longer there to help us find an answer. Hartley Jr. and Dawn were constants in my life during the loss of our home and getting our lives back together. The loss of their father was devastating to them, yet they were and remain, my main source of strength and comfort.

Ironically, after our house burned, I had enrolled in a writing class, *Writing Our Grief*, offered through Lake Superior Writers taught by Deborah Cooper, a chaplain and poet. It was to begin the week Hartley died. I had forgotten about it in the face of my new loss until Deborah, not knowing of Hartley's death, called to see if I had changed my mind. When I told her, she thought it might be too soon for me to return to writing, but I expected it would help me to work and share with writing friends, stories expressing the emotions our various losses evoked. It did enable me to overcome the inertia that made every move an effort.

By the end of the class, I began working on a planned publication of my first collection of memoirs, inspired by the acceptance of one of my short stories soon to be published in a national anthology of memoirs. Remembering Hartley's admonition that I should move on with my life when he was gone, helped me make the effort to pull the broken pieces of my world back together.

I felt compelled to expand my teaching beyond the walls of my church into the community to reach people throughout our long city and encourage them to record their life stories for their descendants. I agreed with articles frequently appearing in periodicals extolling the benefits of legacies of personal memoirs or essays written for children and grandchildren. I contacted the City of Duluth Parks and Recreation Department which managed the Duluth community centers. I proposed to offer the class at these facilities as part of their activity program, which currently focused on recreational offerings. The reaction was positive, and I consulted some of my writing friends at Lake Superior Writers to serve as a steering committee, welcoming their views for implementing the idea. I sincerely appreciated their insight which helped me see this was to be a painstaking process that couldn't be rushed.

I was surprised at how many people from everywhere in the city were able to meet in that one central place to attend my classes, and I continued to work from that mid-town location. I have offered spring and fall classes for over ten years, giving students who have attended any of those classes an opportunity to also work as a group at monthly gatherings. The members, from all backgrounds and ages, surprise their families (and often themselves) with life experiences that become extraordinary in the honest telling. Each is unique, and between the lines we become aware of the courage summoned by ordinary people to survive the challenges they face.

Often, as I begin a new series of classes, I am amazed to find myself in this role I never dreamed of. My sister's voice echoes in my mind, "Today class, we will begin our ABCs," and I remember how it all began. It is the most gratifying accomplishment I can remember—in a way more joyful than writing my own stories. Nothing is more rewarding than hearing a class member read aloud for the first time, and watch it dawn on them that it sounds good to their own ears. Their gratitude prompts me to assure them that our work together has enriched my life immeasurably.

In 2006, I published my first book, *Slices of Life*, with the help of Tony Dierckens, a local publisher. It was followed by

Lake Effect Memories in 2008. Gentle urging by Mara, my friend and mentor, led me to publish stories featuring Hartley that I had been writing through the years, and I had no trouble adding to them from a treasure trove of memories. In 2010, *FORE! The Hartley Stories* was introduced. Tony was my advisor on both the second and third books.

Donna at a reading from the third book *Fore!* with Cyndi Gritzmacher providing musical interludes. Lester Park Golf clubhouse, 2010.

Learning to work around occasional health setbacks, as most people do at my age, I continue living independently. Just when I had thought my life was falling apart with loss of health, home, and husband, I gradually found myself returning to the world of words I had always loved. I am finding this new single life is bringing me a strength and joy I couldn't have imagined possible.

Donna's 2013 writing class at the Copper Top Church on Skyline Drive. Standing L to R: Bob Higgins, Dagney Johnson, Sharon Shuck, Donna, Bonnie Malterer, Marlene Miller, Donna Churchill. In Front: Sue Crawford, Cornelia Dacey, Pat Joyelle.

Rocky Mountain High

With an almost imperceptible whoosh, my skis barely skim the endless expanse of pristine white on this High Alpine run at Snowmass. I am weightless—a feather cruising down the mountain, letting my skis run. It is the only sound I hear; there is not another skier in sight as I approach a favorite viewing place. I traverse to the right side of the run and firmly edge my skis to a halt. Inhaling deeply of the clear mountain air, I survey the majestic Rockies spreading below me in all directions as far as I can see. All is silent now, and I revel in the panorama of glorious formations and colors, trying to imagine their violent beginnings. It is a high point in this Colorado ski trip I am privileged to make each year.

Donna pauses on Snowmass Mountain, Colorado, ca. 1979.

I awake with a start, bewildered—disoriented, to find myself in the blue leather recliner in my own living room. My heart plummets, and I fancy I hear it land with a resonant thud as I realize the year is 2011. The fifty-three year old woman on the mountain top is worlds removed from the seventy-seven year old in the recliner, recuperating from one of the infirmities that accompany aging. I notice my book wedged next to the chair arm, abandoned for the arms of Morpheus as I dozed off.

After the first shocking disappointment marking the abrupt curtailment of my ski trip, I gradually become aware that a warm afterglow remains from that moment on the mountain—I still carry a vivid picture of the woman standing on the sun-drenched peak under the intense blue of a late-winter sky. I know that I have captured the moment in my memory to retain and savor its glowing exhilaration forever, but the woman in the chair has reached a pinnacle far beyond that of the self-absorbed skier. I decide I like the older woman better, and I believe that accounts for my rapidly rebounding spirits.

In 1976 our children were grown and Hartley and I were free to indulge in our favorite activities, which often included outdoor sports. On the rare occasions we contemplated aging, we expected to be playing golf and skiing until we were at least eighty. Our assumption that we would be physically able to do this was brought up short by the challenge of health problems which would prove to continue indefinitely. Perhaps I will always wonder a little if I would have continued to ski into oblivion had this challenging activity not been physically curtailed. I thought I had adjusted to drastic changes in activity, but their reality had returned vividly in dreamland causing me to ponder.

My residual exhilaration remains, and sitting here in my recliner, I continue to reflect on my world. The dream enhances my memory of how my years of varied work experience culminated in returning to the love of writing that began when I scribbled the first words in my little rainbow tablet. I also recall Mother and Aunt Alma, each committed to their prescribed lives, and I know I am in the place I have always belonged. New vistas as wide as the Rocky Mountains opened to me that first day in Mara's 1999 writing class, and today my students and other writers give a richness of purpose to my new life. With an unexpected bonus of the ability to teach, I see my future as a continuing opportunity to share the gift of writing with people whose fascinating stories grace our gatherings as we work to create legacies for descendants yet unborn.

The woman on the High Alpine peak watches with satisfaction—approving, and maybe even envying, the pinnacle from which the woman in the recliner views her world—basking in a glow emanating from her current life that rivals the euphoria often characterized as "Rocky Mountain High."

ABOUT THE AUTHOR

Donna Schilling has lived in Duluth, Minnesota, since July 3, 1942, where her family moved from Long Prairie, Minnesota. She attended Duluth schools and worked in the city for most of her adult life, taking time out to raise her son and daughter.

One Woman's Place is the fourth book she has self-published since she retired from business and began writing memoir and teaching writing classes. She also facilitates a monthly community group for memoir writers.

Her previous memoirs include:

Slices of Life
Lake Superior Memories
Fore! The Hartley Stories

Donna at work in her study, 2013.

Other Books by Donna Schilling